THE TURIN SHROUD
IS GENUINE

THE TURIN SHROUD IS GENUINE

The Irrefutable Evidence

Rodney Hoare

SOUVENIR PRESS

This book is an amended and enlarged version of
A Piece of Cloth, published by Aquarian Press, 1984

First published as *The Turin Shroud is Genuine*
1994 by Souvenir Press Ltd, 43 Great Russell Street,
London WC1B 3PA
and simultaneously in Canada

Reprinted 1994, 1995

ISBN 0 285 63201 9

Photoset by Rowland Phototypesetting Ltd,
Bury St Edmunds, Suffolk

Printed and bound in Great Britain by
Biddles Ltd, Guildford and King's Lynn

Quotations from *The New English Bible* © 1970 by kind
permission of the Oxford and Cambridge University Presses.

Contents

List of Illustrations

LINE DRAWINGS

1

Public Unmasking

S ummer 1988. The Turin Shroud, the linen cloth kept in
Turin Cathedral, which millions have revered for centuries as the shroud that wrapped Jesus' dead body, was being
radiocarbon-dated at last. The public concern was universal.
Many believed fervently that the cloth was genuine, and
expected a first-century result. Many others thought that the
idea of that particular piece of linen lasting for twenty centuries was ridiculous, and expected to learn that it had been
forged in medieval times. A large number disapproved of the
dating taking place at all, feeling that this remarkable cloth
should be allowed to remain a mystery. The cloth would either
be confirmed as first-century or shown to be a medieval fraud,
but there was also a chance of a date between the two, which
would settle nothing. The long summer seemed endless while
the results were awaited.

Two years before, in October 1986, the Pope had agreed
that this final scientific testing of the Shroud could take place.
Seven laboratories had been chosen for the tests, using both
methods of carbon-dating. The tests were to be conducted
under the auspices of the Pontifical Academy of Sciences.
Since then many committees had deliberated, personalities
had quarrelled, and scientific institutions had jostled and
campaigned for the honour of testing the cloth. Eventually
the laboratories chosen were cut to three—one each in Zurich,
Switzerland, Tucson, Arizona, and Oxford. All of them used

the AMS method of testing—accelerator mass spectroscopy. Their results were to be correlated by Dr Michael Tite of the British Museum Research Laboratory.

The technology had to be astonishingly accurate. Professor Hall of the Oxford Laboratory said that their task was the equivalent of finding a slightly different grain in a path of otherwise uniform sand 130 yards wide and stretching from the Earth to the Moon. Yet they expected to achieve that degree of accuracy. Although the AMS method of carbon-dating selected was comparatively new and had not often been applied to linen, the experts sounded completely confident.

Originally it had been planned to announce the results at Easter 1988, but the delays since the Pope's original statement had made that impossible. Even the cutting of the piece to be tested had had to be delayed at the last moment, since on the chosen day Turin had been full of media people covering the end of the cricketer Ian Botham's walk across the Alps.

At 7 a.m. on 21 April, representatives of the three labora-tories, accompanied by Dr Tite, assembled in a side chapel of Turin Cathedral. They found the Shroud already laid out on a table; Professor Gonella and Turin representatives had been there since 4 a.m. extracting the Shroud from its reli-quary and preparing it. The Cardinal was there and television crews. The event had been so badly planned that it then took a full hour for them to decide where the sample from the cloth should be cut.[1] Under the television lights, a thin piece was cut with scissors from the end of the cloth. The strip was taken to a side room by Dr Tite, the Cardinal and Professor Gonella, where it was cut in three pieces which were weighed and put in steel tubes. The same was done with two control pieces provided by the British Museum—one from Egypt, approxi-mately 2,000 years old, the other from Nubia, which archaeol-ogists were sure was 11th–12th century AD. They were selected to be as near as possible to the proposed *genuine* and *forgery* years.

The scientists were able to watch the entire proceedings, except for the half-hour when the strip was taken to the side room for preparing and packing into containers. Not even the videocameras were present then.[2] This was very unfortunate, for some have claimed that there was substitution of different cloth at that stage. Two Germans obtained measured photographs of the three pieces sent out: they did not apparently fit into the piece cut off the Shroud. Nor did they have paired cutting edges. They must have come from another piece of cloth.[3] When I wrote about these allegations to Professor Tite, as he is now, he replied that he could no longer remember the exact shapes cut off for the testing laboratories, but *he was absolutely certain that they came from the piece cut from the Shroud.* His word is good enough for this author.

The representatives from the three laboratories left with their nine steel cylinders and a letter. The one to Zurich, for instance, read:

The containers labelled Z1, Z2, and Z3 to be delivered to representatives of ETH contain one sample of cloth taken in our presence from the Shroud of Turin at 9.45am, 21 April 1988, and two control samples from one or both of the following cloths supplied by the British Museum: First-century cloth; eleventh century. The identity of the samples put in the individual containers has been recorded by a special notebook that will be kept confidential until the measurements have been made.[4]

ETH is short for the Federal Institute of Technology. The Oxford samples were labelled O1, O2 and O3 and the Arizona samples T1, T2 and T3. The letter was signed by the Archbishop and Michael Tite.

To have revealed the details and dates for the control pieces was most unscientific. Control samples should be given blind so that if the experiment then obtains the correct answer, the value obtained for the unknown sample is correct. If an answer is known a temptation exists to skew the results so that the known one is correct.

By the look of the weave the scientists would know straight away which cloth was which, so they knew the answers to the dates of two of the three pieces before even beginning the experiment! As a further control sample they were also given threads from the cope of St Louis d'Anjou which is held in the chapel in the Basilica of Saint-Maximin in France.

After they had gone the Shroud was left for the Poor Clares to repair, stitch to its backing and return to its casket.

Except for those carrying out the tests, the anxious time of silent waiting began. The actual test only takes an hour or so. Why so long a delay? The public was not aware of the long time required by the extremely thorough cleansing and preparation.

The British Museum had received the results from Tucson by 23 June. In early July it was rumoured in the United States that Oxford had proved the cloth to be medieval, and on 3 July the *Sunday Telegraph* also reported that rumour. In fact Oxford had not even started by then. On 22 July the results came from Zurich. Professor Hall in Oxford refused to hurry. He was determined the Shroud should take its place in the queue of work.

At last, in September, Dr Tite had all the results. Having correlated them he sent them to Italy. The Italian post office lost the letter. He prepared another one, but by then the British Post Office was on strike. So it was not until Thursday, 13 October 1988, that the results were announced in London.

The panel facing the press were Professor Hall and Dr Robert Hedges from Oxford, and Dr Michael Tite. On the blackboard behind them was written in chalk *1260–1390!*, and the exclamation mark was later criticised as unscientific. The three testing laboratories had all agreed with that result and the degree of certainty was 95 per cent. Their results for the control samples also matched well. The full results were later published in *Nature*.[5]

There were questions, but the scientists were certain. Professor Edward Hall, who is very direct, said it was definitely a fake, although he supposed some people might continue to believe it is genuine, 'just as there are flat-earthers'. He is reported to have said, 'Someone faked it and flogged it!' but when he was asked how it could possibly have been faked in the Middle Ages, that did not concern him. It was a waste of time worrying about that when we know exactly when it was made. It had to be a forgery.

Sadly, no one shouted 'nonsense'. Many scientists, artists, historians and others who had done research on the Shroud for years were convinced that the carbon-dating had given the wrong result. However, circumstantial evidence was no match for the answer obtained by the one experiment regarded as foolproof by the public in general.

Now, six years later, the time has come to raise the matter again. As a matter of curiosity it is worth investigating the ways in which the stains on the Shroud could have been formed; at the same time, what was the evidence that made the majority of investigators before the carbon-dating think that the Shroud was much earlier and might have been the actual cloth that wrapped the body of Jesus?

2

The Piece of Cloth

I f you go to Turin Cathedral (see plate 1) today you can
see the casket containing the famous piece of cloth behind
thick, bullet-proof glass near the High Altar, but how long it
will be there is uncertain. The adjoining chapel in the royal
palace, built to house it three centuries ago, is being refur-
bished. Strictly speaking the relic should go back when the
chapel is ready, but there are complications and the cathedral
authorities may not release it.

The dilemma began when the former King Umberto II of
Italy died in Geneva on 19 March 1983. In his will he left to
the Vatican a piece of cloth which had belonged to his family
for more than 430 years. Since 1578 that piece of cloth has
been in Turin, almost without interruption. Its ownership was
not seriously disputed until 1946, when King Umberto II was
exiled after a plebiscite and the republic was inaugurated in
Italy. The Shroud remained in Turin, under the guardianship
of the Archbishop.

Since the authorities of the state assumed ownership of other
property of the king, including the palace in whose chapel the
piece of cloth is stored, they might have claimed ownership
of this as well. However, the Italian courts decided that the
cloth still belonged to ex-King Umberto,[1] so presumably it
was his to give to the Vatican. Presumably, but not certainly.
State property was built to house it and is incomplete without

it. That is why the state may possibly require it back when the chapel is prepared for it.

Whether the cloth remains in the cathedral or is returned to the wooden casket with its silver ornamentation[2] (see plate 2) above the altar in the chapel, what matters to most of us is the relic itself. What does it look like? What can we discover from touching and handling it?

When it is taken out for examination, an ivory-coloured material is revealed, with a red backing. The first surprise, perhaps, is its size. It is more than 4.35m (14'3") long, which means it is longer than the main room in many people's houses. It is also about 1.1m (over 3'7") wide. Strange dimensions, but Ian Dickinson has shown that the Shroud was 8 cubits by 2, using the commercial cubit used in the first century.[3]

The material is linen (see plate 3). It feels soft and pliable, and in weight somewhat heavier than shirt cloth.[4] The weave is tight, with the diagonals of a three-to-one twill weave visible—the same pattern used these days for cotton overalls and jeans (see plate 3).[5] What this means is that the weft, which is the thread manipulated by the weaver, is passed alternately over three and under one of the warp threads, the ones that run the length of the cloth attached to the loom. This pattern is very good for resisting creasing and curling, and also wears very well.

The cloth itself is in excellent condition, and the yarn used is remarkably regular. It is pure linen, except for odd traces of cotton on both the warp and the weft threads.[6]

Unfortunately, details such as these cannot date the cloth. Linen lasts for centuries in very good condition. Moth grubs need materials containing keratin to feed on, like wool and feathers, and other insects find the flax fibres too hard.[7] Linens woven about 6,000 years ago can be seen in Egyptian museums,[8] and quite a number of museums in Britain have linen cloths that are thousands of years old.

The regularity of the yarn also does not necessarily indicate recent manufacture. This depends on the knowledge and skill of the spinner as much as anything. The processes take time as well as care, two expensive commodities these days, and the hand-spinners of ancient flax yarns at least matched the regularity of yarn used now.[9]

The three-to-one twill weave should be indicative of the cloth's age, but opinion varies on this point. One author claims that some of the cloths found in the tombs of King Sethos I (*c.* 1300 BC), Ramses III (1200 BC) and Queen Makeri (1100 BC) are woven in the same three-to-one twill pattern.[10] Another reports that three-to-one twill designs in linen are still preserved in the East from a time well before Christ.[11] Yet another denies all this and is unable to find any pre-medieval equivalent of the Turin Shroud.[12] Part of the problem may be the profusion of Egyptian linen cloths of plain weave, preserved by the funeral rites of the Egyptians and the dry atmosphere in the tombs.

There is no doubt that the technology for producing a three-to-one twill in linen existed very early on: it is simply that no examples have been preserved. Woollen textiles with such weaves have been found in Northern Europe dating from the Late Bronze Age, or about 4,000 years ago.[13]

A more significant feature is the presence of odd fibres of cotton, identified as *Gossypium herbaceum*, which, like flax, grows in the Middle East. The importance of this is not simply the presence of the cotton, but the absence of any woollen fibres. Every European loom would have been used mainly for wool, and woollen fibres would have been present in considerable numbers. The cloth, therefore, was not of European origin.

Another line of evidence corroborates this. Plants scatter pollen in abundance, for the chance of any one airborne spore meeting with the appropriate female part of a plant of the same species is very small. The air contains masses of spores in summer, as all hay-fever sufferers know, and they settle everywhere. Microbes then attack them, and after a time only the pollen cases remain. However, these are characteristic of the species and almost indestructible, and they can be used by forensic scientists to determine where items of clothing have been, for instance, following a crime.

In 1969 a Swiss criminologist, Dr Max Frei, pressed some sticky tape on parts of the Shroud and examined the pollen that came off. He found that it was from forty-nine different plants, thirty-three of which grow only in Palestine, Anatolia and the area round Istanbul.[14]

Although precise conclusions regarding the time and place of manufacture cannot be drawn from these facts, some approximate ones can. The cloth was woven on a hand-loom somewhere in the Middle East, probably not Egypt, perhaps Syria or Palestine. The date is difficult to judge. An expert who narrowed it down to the first to third centuries AD[15] may well have been swayed by the result he hoped to achieve. It is just as likely to have been made in the Middle East in medieval times as centuries before that.

While the exact time and place of manufacture are uncertain, there can be no doubt that the Shroud is a beautifully made length of cloth, and probably cost a very great deal. This has prompted the suggestion that it was intended as apparel rather than a shroud.[16] There is a lot of sense to this. A shroud would probably have been made from the simplest weave, which is why the funeral cloths that have been preserved from early times are nearly all plain weave. Garments do not survive so frequently. Incidentally, it is worth noting that this material would have been allowed under the Mosaic Law, for in the Mishna flax may have impurities of cotton. Mixtures of flax and wool were strictly forbidden, however; as it says in Leviticus (19:19), 'Ye shall keep my statutes. Thou shalt not . . . neither shall a garment mingled of linen and woollen come upon thee.'

So much for the material itself. On it, marks can be seen, faint and of a pale sepia colour, standing out from the ivory background.

The most obvious ones are the result of fire damage (see plate 7). For some years before it came to Turin the cloth was kept in the sacristy of the Sainte Chapelle in Chambéry, France. This building caught fire on the night of 4 December 1532 and within a short time the whole chapel was in flames. Two laymen and two Franciscan priests ran in at great risk, broke into the reliquary, grabbed the silver casket containing the cloth and rushed out with it. They must have been terribly burnt, for the casket was so hot that some of the silver melted, falling on to a corner of the folded cloth inside.[17]

The scorches reveal how it was folded then—twice along the length, cutting its width into four, and then again so that it was only one-twelfth the original length. The side of the casket that was hottest scorched the entire length one-quarter from each long edge, the centre and long edges being un- affected as they were on the cool side. Where the molten silver fell, near a bunched corner, small areas of the cloth were burnt right through. The men poured on water to stop the charring.

The results of that night's ordeal can be seen on the cloth in several places. The charred lines running the length have already been mentioned. At intervals along those lines can be seen the patches stitched on by Poor Clare nuns in 1534 to cover the most damaged areas. The other signs are the 'tide marks', which show where the water reached (see figure 1).

The most interesting and important marks on the cloth are along the middle, between the scorches and patches. It is astonishing that these particular stains were not damaged by the fire, and one eyewitness at least, Baron Pingone of Savoy, has described his amazement, when the damaged Shroud was unfolded after the fire, in finding that the crucial stains, which give the cloth its importance, had scarcely suffered at all.[18]

With the naked eye these particular stains can barely be seen. In 1978 the Shroud was on public exhibition in Turin Cathedral, held in a giant frame above and behind the main altar. Filing past it, ten or twelve feet away, I was most sur- prised how little could be perceived. I thought that the bright- ness of the spotlights on it might be partly responsible, and that evening I stayed in the cathedral until the lights had been switched off. The dimness of the stains was still extra- ordinary (see plate 4). The crucial stains were caused by, or represent, the front and back of a naked man's body, the two heads towards the centre of the cloth. To get the two images the body must have been laid on one end, then the other end

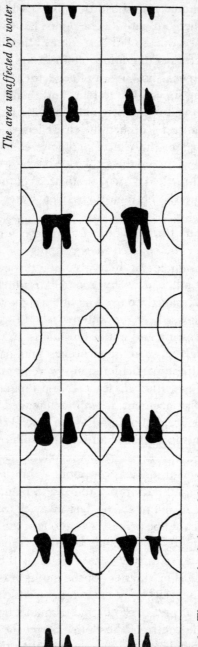

The area unaffected by water

1 *The way the cloth was folded, and the patches and water marks from the 1532 fire. Compare with the positive photograph in plate 11.*

was pulled right over to the feet. This was demonstrated in a painting by Della Rovere (see plate 5).

Even to those who knew what they were looking for during the exhibition, only the few marks of blood, the dim shape of the head, the underneath of the soles, the hands, and one or two other vague marks could be seen. Those who have been privileged to see the cloth close to have also been astonished to find how pale and subtle the image appears.[19] And the closer the eye moves to the cloth, the more mysteriously the image dissolves.

The size of the image is part of the problem, for the stains change in intensity very gradually, so that, when close to the cloth, there is insufficient contrast in a small area for the eye to perceive. Those who are familiar with photographs of the cloth (see plate 11) are particularly surprised by the dimness of the image when they first see the Shroud. They will have seen black-and-white pictures of quite remarkable detail. In them the man stands out from the background very clearly, and minute details of his features, form and wounds can be studied. This is principally because of the characteristics of film. From the first photographs taken in 1898, the sepia has been recorded by film as much darker than the background, so the contrast has been stepped up naturally.

When the main black-and-white photographs, used in research from 1931 onwards, were taken by Giuseppe Enrie, orthochromatic film was used, and older readers will remember how that film used to leave blue skies white while it darkened red so drastically that the lips in a portrait came out black. In fact it is not just with black-and-white film that the contrast is stepped up, for the same seems to happen with colour emulsions.

This vague impression that the eye can discern on the Shroud makes the clarity with which the marks of the man's body are shown in old paintings and engravings of the Shroud, and described in documents, quite extraordinary. The Poor Clares who repaired the cloth after the fire left a remarkably detailed description which, judging from the accounts of modern observers, would be difficult to obtain by eye from the present state of the image. Here is part of their description of the face:

> We noticed, at the left side of the forehead, a drop larger than the others and longer; it winds in a wave; the eyebrows appear well-formed; the eyes a bit less defined; the nose, being the most prominent part of the face, is well marked; the mouth is well-composed, it is quite small; the cheeks, swollen and disfigured, show well enough that they had been cruelly struck, particularly the right; the beard is neither too long nor too little, in the fashion of the Nazareans; it is thin in some places.[20]

Perhaps the intensity of the stains is decreasing with age. With each exhibition the rays of daylight must have turned the background less white, so that the contrast has decreased.

Luckily, if that is the case, modern photographic techniques more than compensate for this. The stains are revealed on photographic prints with a precision yielding far more detailed information to modern researchers than was available to any previous investigators.

However, as a guide to age, neither the study of the cloth itself, nor the details revealed by photography, suggests a date earlier than medieval. The known history of the cloth might.

3

No Proof of Longevity

F rom documentary evidence we know that the cloth now in Turin was moved there in 1578 and has been there almost continuously ever since. Certainty with regard to documentary evidence is impossible, for substitution is always a distant possibility, but in view of the little movement and the religious restrictions, it is extremely unlikely.

The one time it was moved from Turin in the last four centuries was during the Second World War. In 1939 Cardinal Fossati, Archbishop of Turin, had it transferred secretly for safe keeping to the Benedictine monastery of Monte Vergine, a stone fortress at Avellino, some 140 miles south of Rome, which was accessible only by a rough track. There it was kept in a sealed wooden box under the altar, and the monks had orders to take it to a cave in the mountain in the unlikely event of the monastery being bombed. It remained there until 1946. Otherwise, except for the rare occasions when it has been exhibited, it has rested in its reliquary in Turin.

The reason why it came to Turin in 1578 is clearly recorded. The Archbishop of Milan at the time was Charles Borromeo. Intelligent, devout, hard-working, but suffering from a speech impediment, he owed most of his honours and preferment to his uncle, Cardinal de Medici, who became Pope Pius IV and was celebrated for the nepotism he practised.

Charles Borromeo was the first resident archbishop of Milan for more than 80 years. He carried out many reforms, adopted a very simple style of living and gave away most of his large revenue. In times of famine he helped feed the city, and when there were plagues he nursed the stricken. In each case he not only paid for and organised the relief but took part personally. In such high esteem was he held that moves began soon after his death in 1584, which finally achieved his canonisation in 1610.

In 1578 this venerated archbishop, although only 40, was very ill. He had publicly vowed to make a pilgrimage to venerate the Shroud, hoping it would lessen the plague devastating the north of Italy, especially around Milan. The cloth was then kept at Chambéry, across the Alps. To spare him the journey but enable him to fulfil his vow, the Duke of Savoy who owned the relic ordered its transfer to Turin which he was later to make his capital. And there, except for that one short interlude, it remained.

From documentary evidence we can also be fairly sure where the cloth was for some time before it went to Turin. The dates are known during the early sixteenth century when it was exhibited in Chambéry, Vercelli, Nice, Milan and Turin. When French troops were sacking Vercelli in 1553, one of the canons saved it by hiding it in his house.

Much the most important occurrence in the sixteenth century was the fire on 4 December 1532, in the Sainte Chapelle in Chambéry in which the cloth was stored. The scorches and patches resulting from fire damage are now its most noticeable marks.

The Shroud, according to documents, was owned by the Dukedom of Savoy from about 1460. Before that it belonged to Margaret de Charny who inherited it from her father in 1398, and it was his father, her grandfather, who built the collegiate church at Lirey where it was first shown by his widow in about 1357 to make money to pay for the church's upkeep. He had been killed at the Battle of Poitiers in the previous year.

The reason why the Shroud left the church was this. In 1418 a war was being waged in the chapel's neighbourhood, and the priests were very worried about the safety of the Shroud. The church authorities asked Margaret's husband,

Humbert de Villersexel, to protect it in his castle. After his death Margaret guarded it jealously, taking it with her wherever she went on her travels.

When the war was over the priests at Lirey demanded the return of the Shroud, but Margaret ignored them, claiming that her grandfather had only lent it to the chapel. The ecclesiastical court then ordered Margaret to return it. She refused again, and in about 1452 she passed it to the Duke Louis of Savoy, apparently in the belief that it would be in much safer hands with him than with the Church. At the time the Savoy family was known for its piety: Louis had a constant retinue of Franciscan friars and his very beautiful wife, Anne de Lusignan, was equally religious.

There is plenty of documentary evidence to confirm the argument between Margaret and the Church concerning the Shroud. Indeed, for a time she was threatened with excommunication.

There are many gaps in the Shroud's story, years when it is not specifically mentioned, presumably because nothing like a public exhibition happened, but the continuity can be safely assured from approximately the first exhibition in the 1350s, which is confirmed by a pilgrim's amulet.

How certain can we be that the Shroud of Lirey is the same as that at Turin? Pictorial evidence only helps us part of the way back. Photographs prove the Shroud is the same back to 1898. Then we have to rely on paintings and etchings of the Shroud being exhibited. These go back a long way, showing the marks of the scorching from the fire in 1532 (see figure 2 and plate 6). Farther back, Albrecht Dürer's painting of 1516, now in St Gommaire Church, Lievre, Belgium, shows no stains, and finally there is the pilgrim's amulet of about 1356.

However, they all differ from the Shroud in one important respect: they all draw the body images with sharp outlines.

The blurred edges of the image in the Shroud cannot be drawn easily, even by modern artists. In 1898, when copying the image in natural size, Professor Cussetti used an air-brush to obtain the gradual fading of the images into the background. When a photograph was taken of his excellent result, the

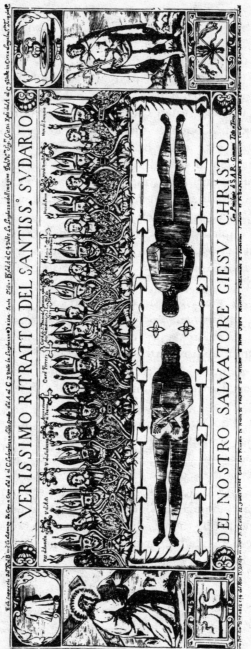

VERISSIMO RITRATTO DEL SANTISS.º SVDARIO

DEL NOSTRO SALVATORE GIESV CHRISTO

2 A sixteenth-century Shroud exhibition. Note how artists copying the Shroud add a loincloth.

photographer noticed there was a sharp border down one side of the face. He pointed it out to Cussetti. 'But how *can* an artist draw a human body without putting down lines?' Cussetti asked. 'So first of all I sketched in all the outlines with a very light touch and then, when the work was completed, I cancelled the lines. In that place I forgot to cancel the line.[1] Why should an originating artist bother to remove the outlines?

There is no surprise, therefore, that the earlier drawings and paintings of the Shroud show outlines of the body. In that respect they are much more like other 'Shrouds' that exist in churches, preserved as relics, with the front and back painted on them in a similar way. They are clearly copies of the Turin Shroud.

This is where the fire damage at Chambéry is so important, for the characteristic shapes of the patches and burns are included on the drawings and paintings of the Shroud being exhibited thereafter. This takes us back to 1532.

However, we can go back even farther, for there are other scorch marks, made when the cloth was pierced by a red-hot rod like a poker. They can be seen most clearly between the dorsal image of the right leg and the edge of the cloth (see plate 7). Perhaps the cloth was subjected to a form of 'ordeal by fire'. These are clearly seen on the painted copy of the Shroud known to have been made by Albrecht Dürer in 1516.[2]

The final pictorial evidence is the pilgrim's amulet to which I have already referred; it was recovered from the Seine and is now in the Museum de Cluny, Paris (see plate 8). Along the top it shows the front and back of a body on a long sheet. Underneath are two shields showing the arms of Geoffrey de Charny on the left, and of his second wife, Jeanne de Vergy, on the right. Between them is a roundel depicting an empty tomb. The pilgrim must have seen the Shroud exhibited at Lirey in about 1357.

From artistic evidence, if the cloth was forged, it must have been manufactured shortly before 1357, so in the early part of the 95 per cent statistical range given by the 1988 carbon-dating. Could Geoffrey de Charny have commissioned a fake Shroud? What do we know about him?

He was a brave soldier and a brilliant general, and his valour in battle earned him many honours. On New Year's Eve, 1349, he was captured by the English while attacking Calais. His king, John the Good, paid the substantial sum of twelve thousand écus to free him and he returned to France in about July 1351. In those days soldiers who were rescued from terrible peril often vowed to go on a pilgrimage or to carry out a pious task. His vow may have been to build a private chapel to house the relic he owned.

He was probably not rich, and the chapel was built of wood and was in bad need of repair within its first hundred years. The money for the dean and canons, 140 livres, was obtained from King John the Good by June 1353. On 28 May 1356, the diocesan bishop, Henry of Poitiers, who comes into the story later, gave the eulogistic address. At this time the inventory of the church's goods did not include the Turin Shroud, which was apparently in a locked box.[3]

Between his release and his death, years busy with almost continuous fighting, Geoffrey became much more religious. He left long verses on the subject of chivalry and piety, clearly visible in his description of the initiation of a knight:

> . . . when one wishes to make a new knight, first it is fitting that he should confess and repent. Then, the day before reception, he should be immersed in a bath, minded that his body should be cleansed of all sin. Then he should go to lie on a freshly made bed with white sheets, which signifies the repose of conscience.
>
> After this the knights should come to dress him in clean linen, symbolising that from this time he should be thought pure and free from sin. Then should be added a crimson garment, which represents that he is prepared to shed his blood to defend the faith of Our Lord. And then he should put on black leggings, as a reminder that it is from the earth that he had come, and to the earth he will return. He should also be girded with a completely white belt, signifying that he would live in chastity . . . Then he should be conducted with great joy to the church, and

there solemnly await daybreak, praying to our Lord that he would pardon the evil days and nights past. And on the coming of the next day they should go to Mass.[4]

This passage suggests he wanted to revive the Knights Templar who had been cruelly exterminated about forty years before, for the baptism, white garments, night vigil, the emphasis on charity and the daybreak Mass probably corresponded to the Templar's reception ceremony.

So to Geoffrey de Charny's death. After an abortive march through France the Black Prince, heir to the throne of England, and his exhausted army reached the area of Poitiers. King John the Good and many of the finest men of France were on their trail. The Black Prince asked if he and his tired men, still marching to the coast, could escape to England, but he was refused. The French, fresh and outnumbering the English by three to one, longed to revenge the disgrace of Crécy.

However, the French knights, who were thrown to the ground when their horses were struck by English arrows at Crécy, decided to march out to fight the English in full armour.

The result was devastating. Beset on both sides on uneven ground against mounted men, the French broke and fled, pursued by the English knights, hacking and slaughtering all the way to the walls of Poitiers . . .

The Prince of Wales penetrated the ranks of the enemy and, like a lion, spared the lowly and put down the mighty and took the King of France prisoner. With the King were one of his sons, an archbishop, thirteen counts, five viscounts, twenty-one barons and nearly two thousand knights. So much potential ransom had never been taken at one time before. Another two-thousand five-hundred knights and men-at-arms were found dead on the field before the English lines, including two dukes. The *oriflamme* itself—the most sacred emblem of France—was barely saved.[5]

The *oriflamme* was the sacred banner of St Denis, a pennant of thin red silk with a cleft end, carried on the end of a lance.

Poitiers was the most devastating defeat in French history.

The knight with the honour of carrying the *oriflamme* had been Geoffrey de Charny, and he had given his life saving the King from the axe of an English soldier.

This gives us some idea of the man who was the first known owner of the Shroud. He must have been a brilliant and gallant fighter to have gained the honour *porte-oriflamme*. As a man he was religious and particularly obsessed with chivalry—indeed all knights of both France and England were obsessed with chivalry at that time. King Edward III instituted England's highest order of chivalry, the Most Noble Order of the Garter, in 1348. The legends of King Arthur and the Round Table were common talk of both nations, and a compilation of the tales was written down in France long before Sir Thomas Malory translated them into the *Morte d'Arthur* in 1470.

Such was the time, and such was the man. The historical objection to the carbon-dating result is that this man could not have perpetrated a fraud. He did not even wish to exhibit it, so what could have been his purpose? Also, if he had wanted the Shroud forged, in all its complexities, would he have obtained for the forger linen which was made in Palestine and which had spent many years there in the open air?

If he did not forge it, how could it have come into his possession?

Before him the last clear mentions of the Shroud were in Constantinople, where a number of reports suggest that it was exhibited regularly in a church over many decades. Then we come to the anxious times after 1200.

A Greek called Nicholas Mesarites, who was keeper of the relics in the Pharos Chapel, had to defend them against a mob in a palace revolution in 1201. He warns the mob: 'In this chapel Christ rises again, and the sindon with the burial linens is the clearest proof.' And later:

The burial sindon of Christ: this is of linen, of cheap and easily obtainable material, still smelling fragrant of myrrh, defying decay, because it wrapped the mysterious, naked dead body after the Passion . . .[6]

He was rather scornful of the material. Not long afterwards, in 1203, Robert de Clari, a French soldier, described a church in Constantinople

> which they called My Lady St Mary of Blachernae, where was kept the *sydoine* in which Our Lord had been wrapped, which stood up straight every Friday so that the figure of Our Lord could be plainly seen there.

Then came the dreadful sacking of Constantinople by the Crusaders. Their leader, Boniface, Marquess of Montferrat, agreed to seize Constantinople and share the city's wealth 'to the honour of God, the pope and empire' and to pay the Venetians. Having entered the city the soldiers were dazzled by the riches all round them. For three days in June 1204 they robbed churches, houses and palaces in a drunken, greedy orgy. Any loose item of value was taken away; if attached to walls, it was torn off. The Crusaders, mainly Frenchmen but encouraged by Venetian sailors, brought mules and carts into churches to load up the sacred relics. Many works of art, too large to take away, were burnt. A prostitute was enthroned in the throne of a religious patriarch and danced and sang to mimic the oriental services.

The Shroud was by far the most valuable relic held by Constantinople and Robert de Clari wanted to find out what had happened to it. He said that, 'No one, either Greek or French, ever knew what became of this *sydoine* after the city was taken.'[7]

The relic completely disappeared from that date until the 1350s. Most of the other relics were transported and given openly to French cathedrals and churches.

Ian Wilson follows an interesting link in his book *The Turin Shroud*. From Constantinople the Shroud may have been taken by the Knights Templar and revered as their secret 'idol', and there is considerable documentary evidence for this. The idol may have been a part, or the whole, of the 'main treasure' kept in the castle at Acre, and then evacuated, through Cyprus, to the new Templar Headquarters near the Louvre in Paris. This idol was a central feature of their worship. Brought in by a priest, it was laid on the altar and the knights prostrated themselves and worshipped it.

King Philip the Fair, a name he hardly deserved from this account, arrested all the Templars at dawn on Friday the 13th, October 1307. The knights were all put to the torture, and most died bravely without saying anything about the well-known idol. Some broke down and described it, a pale and discoloured head with a grizzled beard like a Templar[8]—a fair description of other pictures of Jesus, such as the Byzantine mosaics. The face represented Jesus to the Templars, and they grew beards to be as close as possible to His image.

The leaders were held in prison and tortured cruelly. The king was determined to obtain the idol as well as the wealth of the Order. None confessed where it was. In 1314 the four main masters of the Order were brought to a public scaffold and were asked to make 'confessions' to avoid execution. Two did. The Grand Master, Jacques de Molay, pale from seven years' prison and torture, stood forward and defended the Knights Templar as perfect, though secret, Christians. He and Geoffroi de Charnay, his closest supporter, were led to

a small island in the Seine, situated between the royal garden and the church of the hermit brothers of St Augustine . . . to be burned to death. They were seen to be so prepared to sustain the fire with easy mind and will that they brought from all those who saw them much admiration and surprise for the constancy of their death.[9]

Before the King struck, the Templars had been well aware of approaching danger. In such times valuables are sent to safety to be recovered if the danger passes. Geoffroi de Charnay was very likely a close relative of Geoffrey de Charny. The spelling of names was anything but exact in those days, and each was described with many spellings. In this case the idol could have been passed to Geoffrey de Charny because he was a fine and chivalrous soldier as well as a relative, just the sort of man who would have joined the Knights Templar.

Why did the tortured knights and others describe their idol as a face only? It is possible that the entire Shroud could not be exhibited for fear of the knowledge of their ownership becoming public knowledge; others would be envious and the King might try confiscation. There was another reason why the Knights would find it difficult to worship the whole Shroud, and that was the faintness of the image. If the Shroud, throughout its travels, had been kept in a locked box, with a clear painting on the front of the man's face on the Shroud, the face alone would have become the object of worship. Not only that, but similarly painted locked boxes may have been sent to other Templar churches to be venerated as copies of their sacred idol, and if they had any relics themselves they could have been put inside.

This idea gains considerable support from a find at Templecombe in Somerset in 1944 (see plate 9). Mrs Amy Drew lived in a cottage in High Street, Templecombe, which was clearly, from its title, a centre of the Templars.

> The outhouse was at the back of the house and built into it. You had to step down into it—to get inside. The floor was just earth. I would think it would hold about ten people . . . I had been in the shed many times before, but this time I looked up, and saw part of a face looking down. I just stood there in amazement, looking up. Then on pulling down more of the plaster I could see all the face. It was covered in a thick layer of plaster and very firmly . . .
>
> A workman had to be called to remove it, as it was bigger than it looked up in the ceiling. It was very dirty and covered with cobwebs. But one thing I must point out, the colours were very vivid then, with bright blues and reds.[10]

Unfortunately it was severely damaged by careless cleaning, but it was restored so that the image can be seen on the wood and was unveiled in the church on Easter Sunday, 1956. The purpose of this wooden painting is unknown, but the parish secretary thought it had been the lid of a box.

In The Temple in London and in Cambridge the Templars were in sufficient numbers to build their characteristic round churches, but in the sparser areas round Templecombe the fewer adherents may have come to this outhouse, perhaps in small batches, and enjoyed their ceremonies, each wearing his long white mantle with a small red cross on the left shoulder.

After, or in fear of, suppression, a friend may have fixed the idol in the ceiling above.

There is no certain connection between the Shroud exhibited in Constantinople and the Shroud in the chest at Lirey, but as no other group would have had the wealth and the organisation to have kept that priceless relic for 300 years, it is a reasonable hypothesis. This would suggest that the cloth was formed as early as 1100.

Going farther back still, this idea of the chest containing the Shroud is capable of further application in earlier centuries, and is better studied here than later.

While the Shroud was making its first definite appearance in Constantinople, the Mandylion (see plate 10), which showed the face only of Jesus, was making its last, having first appeared soon after Jesus' death. Ian Wilson's book *The Turin Shroud* tries to show that the Mandylion was the same relic as the Shroud by demonstrating that, by careful folding, only the face could be exposed, and that was the Mandylion. An ingenious theory, but I think it has a flaw. The effect of light over centuries on the face would almost certainly have given a difference in shade between the exposed section and the rest.

However, the very long Shroud could have been placed in a strong box as soon as possible to conceal its existence, and if an early artist had painted on the lid a picture of the face based on the stains, the problem is solved more naturally (see plate 10).

Soon after Jesus' death a mysterious 'portrait' was taken to Edessa by Addai, or Thaddeus, according to Eusebius.[11] It cured Abgar V, toparch of Edessa, of a disease and converted him to Christianity. In about AD 57 Abgar's son came to the throne and persecuted Christians. The 'portrait' was hidden in a niche above Edessa's main gate. Surely it would have been in a box then, rather than the Shroud being placed directly amid the dust? And as the stains on the body were so faint and the tones reversed, the term 'portrait' was hardly justified by itself. So the picture of Jesus may well have been painted on the top of a box in bright colours following as closely as possible the stains on the Shroud. In addition, for centuries there was a reluctance to show Jesus dead, so the picture on top would have had open eyes and looked alive, the bloodstain like a 3 on the forehead translated into wisps coming down from the hair. The Mandylion and the Byzantine pictures show this clearly.

Who painted the picture? According to the fourth century *Doctrine of Addai*, Abgar's envoy, Ananias, painted a portrait of Jesus.[12] If visitors arrived to make a copy, they would certainly have used this rather than the faint, reversed tones on the cloth inside.

The Byzantines defeated the Parthians and captured Edessa, but failed to find the portrait. In AD 525 severe flooding destroyed many buildings in Edessa and, during rebuilding, the 'portrait' was revealed and recognised at once as the original portrait brought to Abgar. In 544 the 'Mandylion', as it was then called, was described as saving Edessa from an attack by the Persian army.

After centuries of scuffles and fights in Edessa the Mandylion reached Constantinople in AD 944. *The sons of the Emperor open the casket and find it extremely blurred.* Replaced again, the Mandylion is carried round the walls of Constantinople and eventually given a permanent place in the Chapel of the Pharos. In 1011 a copy of the Mandylion was sent to Rome which subsequently became the Veronica, *vera icon.*[13]

Here, briefly, is a précis of the broad history of the Mandylion/Shroud.

My suggestion is that if wood could have survived that long, it is possible that only one box may have been the Mandylion for almost a millennium, and then contained the Shroud for many centuries afterwards. The face at Templecombe has many resemblances to the Mandylion. For a short period in

Constantinople .the Shroud was taken out and shown full-length. The Templars returned it to a box—perhaps to the same box, for the Mandylion and the Shroud were in the same chapel. Only the face was exhibited and worshipped. Then, when there were clear signals that King Philip might move against the Templars, it could have been secretly taken to Lirey or fetched by Geoffrey de Charny. Not until after his death was the Shroud removed from the box and exhibited by his needy widow, Jeanne de Vergy, to raise money. Even then, after protests from the Bishop that such a priceless relic could not be in the possession of a poor family, it was returned to its box. In 1389 Geoffrey II de Charny gained permission to exhibit it and in 1398, on his death, it was inherited by his daughter Margaret, as we already know. In times of war she carried the relic around with her, in its box? For centuries the Shroud travelled with the Dukes of Savoy, and when placed in the space above the altar of the special chapel at Chambéry built to house it, the Shroud was in a silver reliquary inside a wooden box. This box must have been irretrievably damaged by the fire of 1532, but a copy was probably made soon afterwards. When the Shroud was evacuated during the Second World War it was again in a wooden box, and perhaps that box remains behind the grille above the altar of the chapel now being renovated, waiting for the silver reliquary to be returned.

Could it have been the same box throughout the centuries up to 1532? Is there a Palestinian wood tough enough? Or were replacements made and the tops repainted?

The painted face on a casket or box is simply a hypothesis, but a more likely one, I feel, than any previous. The prevalence of Middle East pollen supports it, since the Shroud would have been free to the air for long periods up to AD 57, and then in a box except when exhibited. It will remain a hypothesis only unless in Lirey, a Savoy palace, or a chapel or museum in France or Italy, such a casket is found. If the wooden box said to surround the silver reliquary in Turin dates from the sixteenth century, this argument would be greatly strengthened.

4

The Stains

So far we have considered the research done on the cloth. A great deal, however, can also be learnt from a study of the stains on the cloth.

At first sight all the stains, which appear to show the front and back of a wounded man, seem to be the same colour. Only in sunlight is there an obvious difference. Then the marks of blood from his wounds can be seen to be of a red-carmine, quite different from the sepia within the outlines of his body.[1] There is another big difference between the two types of stain. The body-marks, and they will be called that or body-stains in future, reside only on the topmost fibres of the threads, whereas the blood-marks have soaked in between the gaps in the weave and also appear on the back of the cloth. Looking at the Shroud under normal lighting, these points cannot be seen. The images are very faint and almost monotone. Why would an artist have painted it like that?

Two other properties, invisible to the naked eye, show that painting is not merely unlikely but impossible.

The first property was discovered in 1898 when the earliest photographs were taken. When the photographer (see plate 13), Secundo Pia, developed the first plates, he was astonished to find that in the negative the image was incredibly lifelike (see plate 11). The body-stains, which to the eye seem comparatively disjointed, take on an entity, a realism, that is uncanny. It is also very significant, for if a painter is asked to paint a portrait as a negative, and then his attempt is reversed by photography, it never looks as effective as a straightforward portrait in the correct tones. Besides, what motive could a painter have had for doing it in this way, when his masterpiece could not be appreciated until photography was invented many centuries later?

There is a second property the image has which no painter would have given it: the stains contain three-dimensional information. This was suggested for the first time by a Frenchman, Paul Vignon, working from Pia's photographs at the beginning of the century. He realised that the cloth was stained where it was not in contact with the man's body, and the closer it was to the body, the darker the stain. This could not be tested experimentally until the 1970s, when it was done by two USAF captains, Jackson and Jumper. They persuaded a friend of similar shape and size to the body in the stains to lie on a table. By photographing him from the side first uncovered and then covered with a length of cloth, they were able to determine the closeness of the cloth to his skin along the profile. They next measured the darkness of the stain on the Shroud along the same line, using an instrument called a micro-densitometer. When they plotted the darkness of the stain against the distance of the cloth from the body, it gave a neat curve, showing a precise relationship. *The darkness of the Shroud at any point increased with its closeness to the skin,* just as Vignon had suggested. The Shroud can therefore be considered to have three-dimensional information, the z-axis figure (the height) being given by the darkness of the stain.

This was demonstrated beautifully in 1976 by Jackson and Mottern, when a black-and-white print of the Shroud was viewed with a VP-8 Image Analyser. If a picture has this three-dimensional information, the object can be viewed not simply from straight ahead but also, if the machine is manipulated with a joystick, from the sides. To Jackson's and Mottern's delight this is what happened, and they were able to obtain views of the man seen in the body-marks like semi-profiles. The significance of this is very great. A normal photograph or painting does not contain this information at all, and in the Image Analyser will look entirely unreal when an attempt is made to look at it from the side.

Unconnected with the Shroud, it may be of interest to know that there are some pictures that do have this property. For instance, photographs taken by a spacecraft landing on a dark planet with a light beside the camera will have this information: the nearer the object to the light and camera, the brighter it will appear; in this way rocks and boulders can be viewed using the VP-8 Image Analyser as if they were three-dimensional. (It is very difficult indeed to obtain such pictures on earth, but in fact phosphorescent objects photographed through light-attenuating media – a fog is one – give satisfactory results.)[2]

These two scientific properties of the images, the realism of the reversed tones and the three-dimensional information, are the strongest possible evidence that no mortal hand could have painted them. But the scientists have also been interested in the stains themselves.

The investigation of the stains was carried a great deal further in 1978. True, quite a lot of work had been done previously, but it had been piecemeal, often done by scientists chosen on religious grounds. In 1978, after the public exhibition of the Shroud, teams of Italian and American scientists were allowed some time in which to carry out any tests they wished, provided they were non-destructive. The authorities had taken a great deal of persuading to allow the exhibition as well as the scientific examination, and this was a chance which it was felt might not occur again for a very long time.

The American team, called the Shroud of Turin Research Project, which gives the rather ugly acronym STURP, consisted of about thirty high-level scientists with over 8,000 pounds weight of valuable equipment. The frame in which the cloth was to be suspended for the week alone cost $20,000 to construct, and much of the other apparatus was very expensive. In the few days available, the observations of the cloth included direct microscopic observations and photomacrographs; X-ray fluorescence spectrometry; low energy X-radiography; infra-red, visible and ultra-violet reflectance spectra; photo-electric and photographic fluorescence; direct macroscopic visual observations and photographic images in different known wavelength regions, as well as thermal emission images for a variety of wavelengths. Visual transmission, side-lit, and glancing angle photographs were also taken. Material vacuumed from the cloth was examined by electron microscopy and microprobe. Lastly, adhesive tape was applied to the cloth in various areas for later examination by a variety of techniques.[3] Including all these methods 30,000 separate photographs were taken.

Added to previous research, for the Shroud was already by far the most thoroughly researched artefact in existence, such an array of weaponry would be expected to produce conclusive results.

Unfortunately, this did not happen. Partly this was because of the unsatisfactory conditions under which the team had to work. The palace gallery used for the tests was not suitable as a laboratory, having polished wood floors, a highly decorated baroque ceiling and anything but a clinical atmosphere. The nearest gentlemen's lavatory had to be made into the dark-room. There were guards appointed to watch every move made by the scientists, who had no idea how long they would be given to carry out experiments and so could not plan thoroughly.[4] Also, some tests with light or X-rays coming through the cloth were partly spoilt because the backing could not be removed.

Even taking these complications into account, it is surprising that as a result of all the scientists' efforts the situation remained as confusing as it had ever been. A consensus view had been hoped for, but the STURP team proved to be quite unable to produce a formal, agreed report. Instead, groups of members of the team published articles in various scientific journals specialising in their particular fields. The observations they reported were valuable, but their interpretations caused major differences and considerable argument. Not only did the Americans on and off the team quarrel, but the Americans and Italians were just as opposed. At one stage the Italians let it be known that they had proved that the blood-marks on the cloth had originated from real blood, and the Americans were reported as fiercely criticising this, saying that such a result was impossible. A little later the STURP team came out with the same conclusion.

One important factor contributed to the lack of satisfactory results: the composition of the STURP team. It more or less selected itself, the members being mainly pure scientists with little or no experience in dealing with medieval relics. Had scientific experts from museums been included, much more might have been accomplished.

Before summarising some of their results, the terms 'thread', 'fibre' and 'fibril' should be defined. The threads woven into the cloth are quite fine, about one-seventh of a millimetre wide.[5] However, each thread is spun from a hundred or more separate fibres.[6] When a stretch of fibre is separated, by adhering to a piece of adhesive tape, for instance, it is called a fibril. Some of the more important results the STURP team obtained were:

1 Under the microscope, the body-image can be seen to be discontinuous and consists of the yellowing of fibres on the tops of the threads of the cloth. The coloration only goes a maximum of two or three fibres deep into the thread structure. The darkness of the stain depends on how many fibres are yellowed; in other words, the number of coloured fibres per unit area. The affected fibres are coloured to the same extent.

2 Thirty-two adhesive tape samples were removed from a variety of areas on the cloth. It was noticed that the tape came off more easily from non-image than image areas, suggesting that the latter were in some way weakened. There were significantly more yellow fibrils from image areas than non-image, suggesting that they are the dominant visible image element. However, McCrone and Skirius reported that eighteen of the tapes showed sub-micrometre red particles which they identified as Fe_2O_3 of varying degrees of hydration. They found that none of the non-image areas contained these particles, suggesting that they might be a red pigment that was

applied to the cloth either to strengthen the existing image or create it. More will be said of this later. In addition to Fe_2O_3, Heller and Adler found 'blood sherds' and 'blood flakes' on many of the samples. The 'blood flakes' are nearly indistinguishable from the Fe_2O_3 particles optically.

3 Fluorescence tests showed that the plain linen background fluoresced, and the light scorch marks gave a faint reddish brown. However, there was no fluorescence from the body-marks or the blood-marks.

4 The stain-density cloth-body-distance correlation, demonstrated by the VP-8 Image Analyser using the Enrie black-and-white photographs, worked also with the new colour photographs and black-and-white photographs taken on non-panchromatic film.

5 There was no alteration of the image area as it approached the parts of the cloth charred by the 1532 fire. As the silver casket in which the Shroud was stored would probably have melted at 820–850°C, changes should have been detectable had organic dyes or stains been used. Most of the inorganic pigments available during the fourteenth century would also have altered.

6 The water used to extinguish the fire migrated through scorched and unscorched image areas, and no part of the image was apparently water-soluble. The movement of the water was retarded by blood-marks, however.[7]

7 The blood-marks are quite different, thread fibres being matted and cemented together with signs of granules. Red-orange encrustations can be seen between the fibres and in the crevices, with higher concentrations in the valleys at the intersections of warp and weft threads. In places it looks as if such material has fallen away or been rubbed off, leaving exposed the red-orange fibres beneath. The various tests give sufficient evidence to assume the marks were caused by real blood. One interesting result is that some of the blood areas have small fluorescent haloes. These might have been from serum that separated from the blood.

8 There was a considerable amount of 'dirt' on the footprint on the cloth.

Interpreting the stains on the cloth was not what they were interested in, only the composition and properties of the material. Nor were they able to determine the age.

Having presented their observations, the scientists should have attempted a summing-up, and this was where the difficulty lay. On the evidence, the STURP team deduced that the image did not contain coloured foreign matter. They acknowledged that there was possibly a connection between the presence of Fe_2O_3 particles and the image, but felt such a conclusion unjustified from the few tape samples. They did not deny that the particles were there, but felt that they might well have been 'blood flakes' from the blood-mark areas, which had spread when the cloth was folded.

The only explanation of the image formation they felt to be credible, in view of all the experimental results, was that the chemical composition of the cellulose fabric of the linen had been changed in some way. *The nearest approach to the effect of the Shroud image they obtained was by treating some fresh linen with thin coatings of perspiration, olive oil, myrrh and aloes and then baking it gently to simulate ageing.* This matches Vignon's experiments, to be considered later.

The problem arises as to how the gentle gradation came on the cloth, for if by simple contact, there would have been outlined contrast, dark where touching the body and unstained where it did not. An ingenious additional suggestion that sought to explain the three-dimensional information was that the stiff cloth was only in contact with the high points on the body when first applied. Water vapour from the body slowly softened it, until it lay in contact with the whole surface. The stains would have varied if they had been dependent on the time of contact. Unfortunately, this still does not explain why the image did not diffuse through the cloth. It is also extraordinary that the cloth was finally in contact everywhere, in view of the considerable hollows of a normal face. And why, if it depended on the time, was the darkness of the thread stain unaltered, simply the number per unit area?

Some conclusions were certainly achieved. The team felt sure that the blood-marks had indeed been caused by blood. They had a good idea of what the image was, and were confident it did not consist of foreign matter, and was not the work of a forger. How it had been formed was another matter. At the same time the Italian scientists were analysing their observations and continuing their research. Their most important results came from analysis of the blood-marks, for not only were they able to show that the marks must have been formed by human blood, later confirmed by the STURP team, but they also determined its group, AB.[8]

There was nothing very newsworthy in these conclusions, and their impact was lessened by their scattered publication. All the hard work of these many scientists in their several fields barely hit the headlines, which was a pity. What was well publicised was the view of one man, not in the team, who based his opinion on one technique, microscopy, in which he had a well-deserved reputation. But the view he expressed was clear, and newsworthy. It was that the Shroud is a fake, painted in the fourteenth century. Here was the sensation, and he was the investigator who was persistently interviewed when the subject was mentioned on the British media. The memory lingers on and because of this his argument needs to be examined.

5

The Case for Forgery

In spite of the clear evidence that the cloth cannot have been painted there are some, including one very eminent scientist, who feel it must have been, and their case is proved by the carbon-dating. The scientist is Dr Walter McCrone, and his reputation is so high that further examination of the evidence *for* the cloth's having been painted should be examined, particularly in view of the publicity which was given to his opinions.

The amulet showing the first exhibition dated from 1357 indicates that the Shroud must have been forged before that.

The charge of forgery is based on a letter from the Bishop of Troyes, Pierre d'Arcis. He was concerned because the cloth was being venerated by people in his see, although he was sure it had been painted. A predecessor in his post had investigated it. D'Arcis wrote to his pope, Clement VII, about it in 1389. His letter includes the following.

> The Lord Henry of Poitiers, of pious memory, then Bishop of Troyes . . . set himself earnestly to work to fathom the truth of this matter . . . Eventually, after diligent inquiry and examination, he discovered the fraud and how the said cloth had been cunningly painted, the truth being attested by the artist who had painted it, to wit, that it was a work of human skill and not

miraculously wrought or bestowed. Accordingly, after taking mature counsel with wise theologians and men of the law, seeing that he neither ought nor could allow the matter to pass, he began to institute formal proceedings against the said Dean and his accomplices in order to root out this false persuasion. They seeing their wickedness discovered, hid away the said cloth so that the Ordinary could not find it, and they kept it hidden afterwards for thirty-four years or thereabouts down to the present year.[1]

Strong evidence, and if the cloth really was painted, this would have happened just before the first exhibition.

Some qualifications have been expressed about the letter which should be borne in mind.

The Bishop wrote it in a very angry mood. Permission to exhibit the cloth in Lirey, about twelve miles from Troyes, had been obtained from the papal legate instead of from him, the bishop. The reason is not known, but it may well have been because of the previous animosity between the canons and the bishop, so that he would have played any card he could to defeat them. His description of his predecessor's actions seems surprising, since the former bishop gave his confirmation of the establishment of the church in Lirey on 28 May 1356, bestowing his unqualified and lavish blessings. This would have been after his discovery that the cloth venerated there was a forgery! Note also that the Pope, in response to Bishop d'Arcis' letter, did not stop the exhibition, but insisted on two occasions that the bishop remain 'perpetually silent' on the matter, on the second occasion threatening excommunication.

Another reason may have been the crowds drawn to Lirey. Troyes Cathedral gained a considerable revenue from collection boxes put beside its relics, as well as the general collections. Among these relics were some obtained from the loot of Constantinople, including remains of St Helen of Athyra, a fragment of the True Cross, the skull of St Philip, the arm of St James the Great and a dish used at the Last Supper.

The year the letter was written by the Bishop was 1389, when funds were badly needed for the restoration of the upper nave of Troyes Cathedral after a collapse. The Bishop may well have been looking with envy at the large numbers of pilgrims being drawn to Lirey, a humble collegiate church not far away, to see the Shroud exhibited there.[2]

If the former bishop did locate an artist who claimed to have painted the Shroud, there is a possibility that he had painted one of the other shrouds that were venerated in Europe at the time rather than the Turin Shroud. He would have copied it from the Shroud in that case; most fakers did.

The letter quoted is not the only reason why many historians say the cloth must be a fake. They also deduce this because for many centuries before the fourteenth its location is not precisely known. To a scientist that is no proof whatsoever that it cannot be genuine. If an old pot is dug up, a painting found in an attic, an ancient scroll in a Jerusalem bazaar, the items are examined by experts scientifically. If, as a result of the most careful tests, the pot is pronounced to be Roman, the painting an unrecorded Rembrandt, the scroll one from the Essene community beside the Dead Sea, no one says, 'They can't be! We have no idea who the owners have been for centuries. They have no history whatsoever. Therefore they are fakes!' Similarly if some painted linen hangings are found in 1894 which appear medieval, back to the period when artists painted only on wood or walls, and the experts are sure they are painted by Guido da Siena, their view is accepted without question. The same standards apply to the Shroud: examine the material, analyse the marks on it, and let the cloth tell its story.

It is interesting that Dr Walter McCrone should be the scientist who is doubting the authenticity of the Shroud, for he was involved in a classic examination of a similar kind some years ago.[3] In 1957 an American book dealer bought from an Italian bookseller in Barcelona a map, known as the Vinland Map. It was apparently drawn by a monk from the Upper Rhine during the fifteenth century, and it showed that Leif Ericson visited America about 500 years before

Columbus. It was most authentic in appearance, and worm-holes in it exactly matched those in two well-known medieval documents, suggesting that it had been bound with them. After Yale University bought it, they sent it to the British Museum for non-destructive testing, and it was found that the map did not quench fluorescence under ultra-violet light as the other two documents did. So the map was sent to Dr McCrone for further testing. Removing less than a microgram he discovered evidence indicating that while the parchment was genuinely of medieval date, the ink contained a syn-thesised pigment, anatase, not developed until about 1920. The map, he claimed, was a fraud.

And now Dr McCrone was claiming the Shroud image was painted. What was the evidence?

Dr McCrone was able to study 32 tape samples brought back by the STURP team from the 1978 examination. The tapes had been pressed against the cloth in many different places, including unaffected linen background, scorch areas, body-marks and blood-marks. As a result of his examination, he was soon saying that the Shroud image has two constitu-ents: uniformly coloured linen fibres and iron particles. The nature and origin of the coloured fibres was unknown, but the iron oxide was a mixture of red and yellow pigment particles (pure Fe_2O_3 and hydrous Fe_2O_3 respectively). None of the control samples, where there was no image, showed these red particles, whereas all the blood-mark ones did, as well as two-thirds of the body-mark ones. He concluded that there was a direct correlation between Fe_2O_3 particle concentrations and image areas, and suggested that they had been intention-ally added during the past 200 years.

To demonstrate how the iron oxide would have been applied to the cloth without any of the directional indications that are obtained with brush strokes, McCrone rubbed his finger in some powdered jeweller's rouge, transferred it to a piece of paper until there was very little indeed left on his finger, and then used that to apply to a piece of linen.[4]

His claim caused considerable opposition from the STURP team and Turin. He did not retract in the least, but gave a clear description of his methods and findings, and revealed further conclusions. The iron oxide particles were now reckoned much more like the artist's pigment known as Venetian or Indian red than the jeweller's rouge. Not only that, but they were very closely attached to the fibres, sometimes in clumps within a transparent gel. Applying the agent amido black, he obtained a fine blue stain round these clumps of oxide. This indicated that a protein material had been used as a weak medium, a tempera made from collagen. As he found this on the body-mark and blood-mark areas, he concluded it must have been put there by man. To account for the three-dimensional information, Dr McCrone suggested that the artist tried to portray a shroud rather than a portrait of a man, so formed the image by working from the contact points where the cloth would have touched the skin.

In conclusion Dr McCrone stated:

> Our work now supports the two Bishops and it seems reasonable that the image was painted on the cloth shortly before the first exhibition, about 1357. It is, however, possible that the image and/or the cloth is at least as old as about 1350, that it was done by an artist and that if all iron earth pigment plus tempera medium were removed there would be no image on the 'Shroud'.

The STURP team did not agree at all with Dr McCrone's conclusions, and they were using a very wide range of techniques.[5] Two members of the team, Heller and Adler, studied the fibrils with a microscope as Dr McCrone had done, and their observations were quite different. They reported on the modern debris with the fibrils—insect parts, wax, modern synthetic fibrils, red and blue silk, wool and felt tip pen dye marks. The red and blue silk fibrils were seen with almost every sample, and presumably came from backing cloths with frequent folding and unfolding. As has been mentioned, they also found 'blood sherds' and 'blood flakes' on many of the samples, which were almost indistinguishable from the comparably-sized Fe_2O_3 particles optically, so that the possibility arose of mistaken identity. There could have been a dispersion of these blood remains whenever the cloth was folded and unfolded, spreading the particles to other areas.[6] In addition to this, painted copies of the Shroud were pressed against the real Shroud to pick up the grace of the original. Some Fe_2O_3 could well have been transferred.

There were many other tests, and some of Dr McCrone's conclusions were criticised. His amido black test had been positive only for the blood-mark areas, for instance, so that there was no clear indication that protein-based tempera was on the body image. Nor is amido black the best test, according to others, as it stains cellulose so easily that false positive results may occur. The further tests carried out by STURP members showed that the discoloration of the yellow fibrils did not come from any likely organic or inorganic pigmentation. The STURP team's conclusion that there was no pigment on the cloth was derived from a far wider selection of analytical methods, and this was placed against Dr McCrone's clear mastery and superior experience in his own field.

However, Dr McCrone's authority was decreased recently when the veracity of his 1974 investigation of the Vinland Map was questioned. His examination of 29 microparticles removed from the map had suggested that titanium-based inks, containing anatase, were used. To test his conclusion a number of scientists at the Crocker Nuclear Laboratory in the University of California used a proton milliprobe to examine the map. This is a non-destructive method. The high energy proton beam is focused on the thin ink line, generating X-rays, and these reveal elements, from silicon to uranium, that are based in the ink. A wide variety in the inks was discovered, but the titanium was in very small quantities, far smaller than would be expected had modern inks been used. The highest concentration was found not only in the 'Vinland' region, but in 'Spain', 'Tunisia' and 'Japan'. After comparing their findings with readings taken on genuine old parchments, the scientists affirmed that McCrone's interpretation that the Map is a twentieth-century forgery must be re-evaluated.[7]

His use of only microscopic evidence to prove the Shroud is a forgery is similarly contradicted by other scientists using a much wider range of investigations, so that the scientific argument looks less impressive than the historical evidence for the Bishop of Troyes' letter.

There is also the common-sense view in favour of the cloth having been painted, which most people form when first hearing of the Shroud. Surely it cannot be two thousand years old, as it is claimed to be? Most likely it was painted for some religious purpose in medieval times, when relics were being produced by the hundred. Since there were more than forty purported shrouds around at one time, this one is probably as false as the rest.

However, the arguments against the cloth having been painted, apart from the scientific, are remarkably powerful. Some of them are:

1 The painting is so faint that the gradation cannot be seen when close enough to paint it. Only by standing some feet back can its effect be seen.

2 The anatomy of the body is perfect, right down to small details like the separation of serum from blood. It is unlikely that an artist even now would paint with such accuracy.

3 The blood-marks were caused by real blood. Also the fibres underneath them are not stained yellow. The blood-marks were therefore applied to the cloth first and prevented the body-stains from appearing there. An artist would have applied the blood-marks last.

4 No medieval artist would have been able, nor did he have any reason, to paint a negative image which would give a perfect positive on reversal centuries later when photography enabled this to be seen.

5 A medieval artist would have used a brush, and the direction of the brushmarks would be detectable with a microscope. No directions of brushmarks can be seen.

6 No painting has the three-dimensional information revealed by the VP-8 Image Analyser.

7 A European artist would not have troubled to obtain linen that could only have been made in the Middle East, and which had pollen on its surface from long exposure there.

8 The places and directions of the stains must have resulted from details of crucifixion not known by medieval artists. (The position of the nail wound, no sign of thumbs and the use of a *sedile* on the cross—covered in the next three chapters.)

9 Medieval painters, and indeed nearly all painters up to the middle of the nineteenth century,[8] worked from outlines, whereas the Shroud contains an extraordinarily soft gradation from image to background.

10 Assuming that the painting must have been a religious one and represented the shroud of Jesus Christ, until comparatively recently artists have always painted Jesus with a halo and wearing a loincloth.

11 Medieval paints would have cracked on folding and would have changed nature close to the heat of the 1532 fire.

12 The material appears to support itself fairly stiffly between the knees, hands and abdomen, and across the hollow between the chest and chin. On the other hand, there is more contact widthways around the arms, legs and body. The drape is stiffer lengthways, along the warp, than widthways, along the weft. To a materials expert[9] it would be astonishing for an artist to represent drape so correctly.

13 The presence of dirt where the bottom of the foot is represented is an unlikely touch of realism for a painting.

14 An artist would have painted thumbs as well as fingers, but none are visible on the Shroud. If a nail is hammered between the wrist bones of an amputated arm in the place indicated by the blood-stains, the thumb is drawn across the palm and would be invisible from the back of the hand.

15 One last point. The author has managed to trace only one

painting of the period made on linen rather than wood. This is the Lenten hanging in the Siena Pinacoteca, having come there from the Pieve di Santa Cecilia, Crevole, in 1894. Its earlier history is unknown. It was painted by Guido da Siena, probably in the 1270s. The three sections are the *Transfiguration*, *The Entry into Jerusalem*, and *The Raising of Lazarus*. Only a photograph of *The Raising of Lazarus* is reproduced in this book (see plate 12). You cannot see the bright colours, unfortunately. However, note the haloes, the sharp outlines, the incorrect anatomical dimensions. See Lazarus in the graveclothes described in the Gospels: no artist would have painted Jesus naked or dead.

The case rests. As the arguments stand at the moment, those who maintain that the cloth could not have been painted seem to have a far stronger case. But if it was not painted, then some natural process, using a human body, must have caused the stains.

6

A Natural Process?

P aul Vignon has already been mentioned as the man who first suggested that the darkness of the stain decreased with the distance of the cloth from the skin.

Born in 1865, the year the Matterhorn was climbed, Vignon was attracted by the magic of climbing, with thousands more, and he was very good at it. He had plenty of inherited wealth and could take up any hobby he pleased.

L'Aiguille Meridionale d'Arves is a very difficult climb consisting of a 10,000-foot ridge with steep flat slopes each side. Vignon, in his early twenties, was the first to climb it. He continued to climb peaks with such frantic energy that he overdid it, and in a long convalescence he became a considerable artist.

Not long afterwards he happened to meet an agnostic, Yves Delange, and was persuaded to study biology in which he soon shone. When he heard of the first photographs of the Shroud taken by Secundo Pia in 1898 (see plate 13), he decided to apply all his knowledge to investigating the Shroud himself, for he was a devout Catholic. After travelling to Turin to meet Pia, he brought back large positive and negative prints. The full account of his work then can be read in his book *The Shroud of Christ*, published in 1902.

The major marks on the cloth have already been mentioned. They are the scorches and patches from the 1532 fire, and the stains caused by the front and back of a man's body, on which can be seen blood-marks from his injuries. Closer examination of the photographs reveals many important details.

The face is best seen on the negative, for with the tones reversed it is remarkably lifelike (see plate 14). The man has a thin, rather old face, his hair coming down each side, with a majestic expression. The left side of his face looks rather buffeted, particularly just below the eye, and his nose appears swollen on one side. The streaks of blood are better seen in the positive. The most obvious one, just above the left eye-brow, has the shape of a 3 (reversed in the positive) with an extra drop just below its base. Other streaks of blood come down the hair, and they are all round the head, a cluster of them clearly visible on the back image.

The main blood-marks on the body (see plate 15) are on the forearms, the left wrist, a big one on the right side of the chest running into a patch from the fire, a series of trickles going right across the back above waist height (see plate 7), under the soles of the feet on the rear image and on the toes on the front image. The wounds on the hand and feet suggest the man suffered crucifixion. The blood-marks on the left hand are in the shape of a V, the point issuing from a place on the wrist rather than the hand itself. Under the feet the blood apparently issued from the middle of the soles, some blood running to the toes, presumably when he was suspended upright, and some to the heels when the body was laid down. There is a jagged blood-mark on the cloth beside the right heel. Trickles of blood also come across the left arm and along the right arm.

The body-marks are delicately shaded, and match the shape of a body except for a few details. The shoulders and neck do not appear on the front image, perhaps because the cloth was held too far away from them, and the same is true for the bottoms of the shins. The right wrist is obscured by the left one which covered it, and although the fingers on both hands can be seen clearly, neither thumb is there. The left shoulder-blade appears rather dark, as if rubbed or bruised. But the main surface marks are shaped like small dumb-bells, and they can be seen all over the back, buttocks and legs, and even on the front image in places. It has been suggested that these are scourge-marks.

Knowing nothing of carbon-dating, Vignon assumed from the evidence that the victim must have died before the fourth century, when crucifixion was finally outlawed in the Roman Empire. The Romans usually scourged victims before attaching them to crosses. The *flagrum* they used for this had a short handle, with several long thongs or chains attached. Near the end of these thongs were fixed pieces of bone or lumps of lead, to bruise and bite into the flesh, adding to the agony and weakening effect. Two of these, wielded by men on each side of him, could have made the marks seen on the man in the Shroud (see plate 16).

Vignon felt at first that the image might have been painted, but the realism of the negative argued against this. To make sure he painted linen as near as possible in weave and weight to the Shroud with very thin images of watercolour and oils. As soon as the paint had dried, bending the linen caused the paint to crack. He was the first to point out that apart from the difficulty of working in reverse, why should a medieval painter have attempted it when the worth of his art could not be appreciated for many centuries? But Vignon realised that there was also the possibility that an artist had painted it normally, but that in time chemistry had altered the paints, reversing their tones, as had happened to a fresco in Assisi. In the only case known, sulphur had acted on the lead base of the paints causing this inversion; but in the case of the Shroud the image is of one colour only, so Vignon concluded that this explanation would not be possible. In addition, inversion could only occur with solid paint, and there was no evidence of any paint on the cloth at all.

Vignon found further evidence against painting in the blood-marks. They are clearly outlined. A liquid placed on the cloth would have spread along the threads, leaving jagged edges, so that a forger would have used either thick paint for the blood, which would have come off with frequent folding and unfolding, or some sort of stain, which was unlikely if not absurd. Vignon the biologist next studied the blood-mark

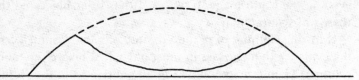

3   *Vignon's section through a drop of blood which has dried on an impermeable surface.*

above the left eyebrow. It starts with a wound not far below the hair.

> The blood which has flowed therefrom has met in its course the two wrinkles of the forehead, and has, by this slight opposition, been forced to spread itself out, forming two small horizontal pools; thence it continued to flow, until it ended in a tear of blood close to the eyebrow, and having thus flowed, it dried upon the skin.
>
> Now any drop of blood, drying thus, upon a substance into which it does not penetrate here, takes, when coagulated, a sort of basin-like shape, a section of which we give here.
>
> The border or brim of the basin is formed by the fibrine of the blood, containing the red corpuscles in its coagulum; the centre is composed of the serum, which in drying takes a dull brown tint. Here, as the liquid part of the serum evaporates, the convexity of the centre is depressed. The contour of the drop of blood preserves, however, the same shape as when it was fresh.
>
> Now this description applied exactly to the blood-drop on the forehead.[1]

Vignon studied the other blood-marks, and found further evidence that the accuracy of the image was astonishing, and far beyond the knowledge of any painter in medieval times. He felt that this particularly applied to the blood-mark on the left hand.

> The nail-wound of the left hand is in the wrist, not in the centre of the palm as demanded by tradition. In a

forged relic such a parade of independence would scarcely have been tolerated. As it was, to have shown the public only one hand, and consequently only one wound, was remarkable enough. Such licences would be pardoned only in the most authentic relic. Yet anatomy proves that the nails must have been driven into the wrists, not into the hands. Here again tradition is contradicted.

What would have become of the body on the cross, had the nails been driven through the palms of the hands? The weight of the body would quickly have enlarged the wounds, and the ligaments at the base of the fingers would soon have given way. If, however, the nails were driven in at the wrist there would be no chance of the wound's enlargement; indeed the very weight of the body would throw pressure on the extremities of the metacarpal bones, which are very firmly united.[2]

Vignon describes this feature with a scientist's exactness, and may have felt that no one had noticed it before him. Surprisingly, it was mentioned as early as 1598, in the first book written about the cloth. The author, Monsignor Palleotto, described how the nail went through the hand at the spot 'where the hand and forearm join, known to the doctors as the carpus'. He also pointed out that nailing through the palms would not have been possible as 'they would not sustain the weight of the body, but would tear, as is confirmed by the experience of painters and sculptors who have studied corpses.'[3] Painters of the Renaissance had the knowledge to paint it correctly, and Van Dyck and Rubens are among those who showed nails going through the wrists of the crucified victim, so this particular detail cannot be used as a strong argument against forgery later than approximately 1400.

The narrowness of the face image interested Vignon, and also the way the hair was held up beside the cheeks, and he suggested there must have been cushions or similar supports placed on each side of the head. In that case the cloth would not have fallen round the edges of the cheeks, which would have given a wider image, as he illustrated with a diagram.

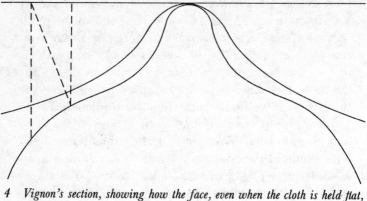

4   *Vignon's section, showing how the face, even when the cloth is held flat, appears narrow.*

Apart from holding the hair up, it would also account for the way the shoulders do not appear in the front image, for those same cushions would have held the cloth away from them.

Vignon's detailed description of how the stains in particular areas were formed makes fascinating reading. But he is best known for his attempts to discover the general process by which they were transferred to the cloth.

Once he had eliminated painting as a method of forging, he wondered whether a live body could have been used. Wearing a false beard, he put red chalk on his skin and lay on a laboratory bench. His assistants then placed on him a length of linen coated with albumen and attempted to pick up the chalk impression of his body. The results were grotesque compared with the original. Nor was there any way of obtaining a delicate gradation. If the cloth did not touch the body at any point, nothing was picked up there. The skin could not transfer the solid to the cloth across a space.

It was this that fascinated Vignon. He did manage to obtain a negative by this method, but a very rough and coarse one, whereas the print on the shroud

is a still more perfect negative, because the image has been also in part produced without contact. Nevertheless we do not pretend that this negative is as true a one as if it had been taken by means of a lens . . . In the language of science it is the result of action at a distance (that is to say without contact); geometrically speaking it is a projection.[4]

This action over a distance meant that the stains could not have resulted from the transfer of a solid or a liquid from the skin to the cloth. It had to be a gas. So Vignon, and a colleague, René Colson, set out to find what gas it could have been.

They first investigated oriental burial customs and found that aromatic substances, especially myrrh and aloes, were pounded up in pure olive oil for use as an unguent. This could have coated the cloth. Experiment showed that only when the gas ammonia came in contact with the treated cloth, just the right colour stains were formed in time. They then had to find out when a body can give off ammonia.

Ammonia occurs as a final product of the fermentation of urea. Urea is mainly discharged by the body in urine. That is why mothers are affected by the pungent fumes of ammonia when they change wet nappies that have been worn by their babies for some time. But urea is also discharged in very small quantities in perspiration. Normally there would be too little urea exuded to have any effect, but Vignon was delighted to find:

that *in morbid sweat* the increase of urea is quite astonishing. M. Gautier says: 'Urea may be produced so abundantly in certain morbid sweats that it forms crystals on the surface of the body. A fringe of such crystals has been seen on the forehead where it joins the hair, presenting an appearance like down' . . . M. Gautier also personally assured me that viscous sweat strongly charged with urea would be given off by any fever patient in a crisis of pain. Further—and this is of great importance—a man who has been tortured for a length of time will at death be found to have his body covered with a deposit rich in urea. This deposit left after the heavy sweating, caused by acute pain, has somewhat evaporated. The skin would remain moist. If, then, after death such a corpse were covered with a sheet soaked in aloes, the urea would ferment, carbonate of ammonia would be produced, ammoniacal vapours would arise; these vapours would oxidise the aloes, and would reproduce on the cloth a negative by chemical action.[5]

It seemed to tie up very well. There were some slight snags. Vignon tried to use this process to obtain a reasonable stain on cloth from a plaster head of Michelangelo and failed. However, he did manage a good one of a hand if he let the ammonia filter up through a glove, but why the glove was necessary was not clear.

However, the chemistry seemed to fit in so well, and the abnormal exudation of urea in the sweat of a tortured man was such an extraordinary coincidence that Vignon's vaporographic theory, as he called it, had considerable support after his book was published. The doubts came later.

As well as being a brilliant scientist Vignon was a first-rate artist, and in the 1930s he turned to another aspect of the Shroud. Show people the face on the negative of the Shroud and they usually say that it looks just like Jesus. They say this because they have seen paintings of Jesus' face. And Vignon investigated just how long Jesus has been portrayed as looking that way.

For the first five centuries Jesus is represented in a variety of ways—as a shepherd, teacher, fisherman and leader of a dance—with different shapes to his face and usually shaved (see plate 17). Then, suddenly, the Byzantine mosaics show Christ with the face with which people are familiar. Nor is it just the shape. Vignon listed oddities on the Shroud face such as the hair and forked beard, a transverse streak across the forehead, the buffeting of the nose and right cheek, two small strands of hair emerging onto the top centre of the forehead, the characteristic V shape between the eyebrows and the unusually wide eyes. These, he found, were on the Byzantine representations of Jesus and quickly spread as the accepted likeness elsewhere (see plates 18 and 26).

The conclusion he drew, and it is difficult to disagree on seeing the evidence, was that the Byzantine artists had seen the Shroud being exhibited and as a result this became the acknowledged image of Jesus. In fact the Mandylion had been discovered by the Byzantines in 525 and their artists copied the portrait 'not made by human hands'.

The strong resemblance of the portraits to the face on the Shroud is the artistic objection to the carbon-dating result.

1. Crowds round the doors of Turin Cathedral during the 1978 Shroud Exhibition.

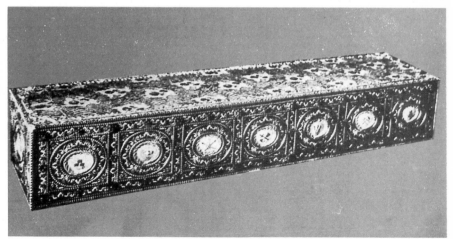

2. The silver reliquary that holds the Shroud when it is not being exhibited.

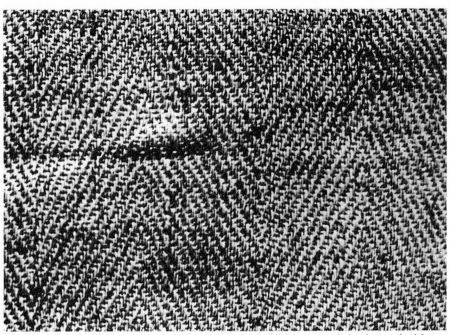

3. Close-up of the cloth. Note the herring-bone pattern, and the irregularities.

4. The Shroud in its bullet-proof frame for the 1978 exhibition.

5. Painting by Della Rovere (*c.* 17th century) showing how the Shroud was folded round the body to get its two images.

I Luero Ritratto del Santiss. Sudario, dedicato alle Altezze Sereniss: di Maria Adelaide, Maria Anna e Maria Lodouica Princi. pesse della Real Casa di Sauoia, in questa prima Impressione. *dall' Vmilis, e osseguiosiss. Seruitore* Pietro Antonio Boglietto in Torino

6. Seventeenth-century exhibition of the Shroud in the presence of the princesses of the House of Savoy. *By kind permission of Sherborne Castle Estate*

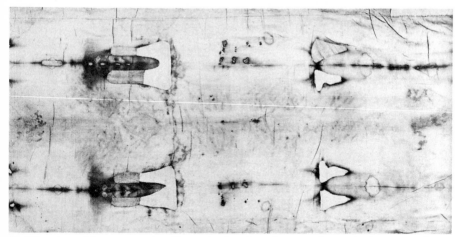

7. The dorsal image on the Shroud, showing the scorch marks between the right leg and the edge of the cloth. Note also the even staining over the whole image area, suggesting that the body could not have been lying on a hard surface.

8. Pilgrim's amulet, *c.*1357. The top section with its front and back figures represents the Shroud, above the arms of Geoffrey de Charny and his wife on either side of a roundel showing a tomb. *Copyright Musée de Cluny, Paris*

9. The Templecombe panel showing the face of Christ. Found hidden in the ceiling of a shed, the panel with its faint image is now in a frame with a substitute board for the missing top one. *Courtesy of Ian Wilson*

10. A Mandylion, showing the face of Jesus only. Formerly in the possession of the Dukes of Jaroslav, this one became the battle emblem of the Russians. Now in the Tretyakov Gallery. Late 13th/early 14th century. *Courtesy of Ian Wilson*

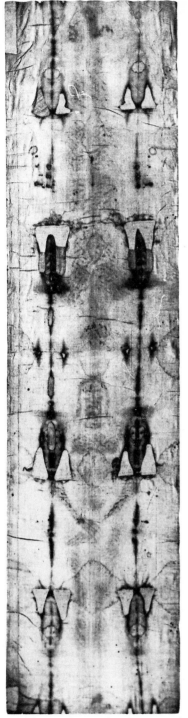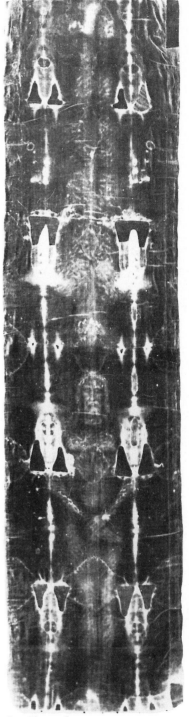

11. Positive and negative images of the entire Shroud.

12. 'The Raising of Lazarus', one of the panels of the Lenten Hanging, painted by Guido da Siena, *c.*1270. Formerly in the Pieve di Santa Cecilia, Crevole, it has hung in the Siena Pinacoteca since 1894. *Copyright Conway Library, Courtauld Institute of Art*

7

The Thermographic Correction

The vaporographic theory of Vignon seems very persuasive. The extraordinary way in which ammonia can be produced by the body from urea under duress seems such a coincidence that it must surely be true. But there are snags, and the theory soon lost favour. The first problem is caused by the gradation. The logic that the agent must be a gas rather than a liquid or solid, since it acts over a distance rather than by contact, seems incontestable. However, if it is a gas, how does its effect decrease with the distance to the cloth? The volume of gas between the body and the cloth would be comparatively small. Any gas emitted by the body would soon become of uniform density in that volume, the gas diffusing through the cloth at the same rate as it was generated on the skin. There would be no question of gentle gradation, therefore. Vapours diffusing through space do not travel in parallel lines, nor do their densities decrease with distance.[1] In view of the small volume between the cloth and the skin, the density of the gas would have been practically constant throughout the volume and so the stain would have been uniform: for instance, there would not have been the gentle gradation above the eyes.

The second main objection has also been indicated, for as the gas diffused up through the cloth the reaction would have continued, whereas only the closest fibres of the closest threads have been stained.

The STURP team also eliminated the theory on less important grounds, principally because they could find no trace of the products expected from the ammonia-aloes reaction.

However, I began my research well before STURP was born, and having read Vignon's 1902 book.

Wishing to know more, I obtained negative and positive three-foot photographs of the Shroud and considered who would be best qualified to interpret the information they contain. Forensic scientists, surely. However, they were not in the telephone directory and reputed to be impossible to contact. I then had two pieces of great fortune. I rang 999, the emergency number, and asked for police. A constable answered.

'I have here,' I told him, 'photographic evidence that a crime may have taken place. I daren't accuse anyone without forensic scientists confirming my suspicions.'

A pause, and then, 'Right, sir. The number you need is . . .'

That was the first stroke of luck. The second came when I rang that number. Mr Norman Lee, the Director of East Midland Forensic Science Laboratory, answered.

'I have these photographs,' I started, 'and I think they may be evidence of a murder.'

'What are the wounds?' he asked.

'Well, it looks as if this man has been stabbed through the chest.'

'That didn't necessarily kill him. Even if it went into his heart.'

'He has also been pierced through his wrist.'

That was all I said before, after a pause, he said, 'Now look here. When do you think this crime took place?'

I had hoped he would not guess. 'About two thousand years ago, actually. But listen! I think you'll find this very interesting.'

'Where did you get these photographs?'

'They are photographs of the Turin Shroud, which I think may be genuine.'

He thought, and thought. 'Well,' he said, with a smile in his voice, 'bring them here on Friday at ten. We'll have a brief look at them for you. I'll tell you how to get here . . .'

How great my luck had been was emphasised when I read of the attempts of an American to contact the crime experts in the FBI. Back came the sort of letter only a civil servant of many years could produce:

> Our normal policy requires that the FBI laboratory con-
> duct examinations of evidence in criminal cases for all
> duly constituted law enforcement agencies. Although
> exceptions to this policy are possible, it has been found
> that examinations of the type you requested from photo-
> graphs are not productive. Examination of the original
> material would be a more appropriate procedure; how-
> ever, since such material is in the custody of another
> country, it is not within the province of this Bureau to
> conduct such examinations.[2]

At the appointed time I knocked on the door and Mr Lee came to meet me. We climbed some stairs to enter a large laboratory where white-coated scientists were working at laboratory benches, many looking down microscopes. As they saw me they gave me a broad grin.

'OK. Here he is,' called Mr Lee, and he led me along to a large bench which must have been used for bodies. The others, still smiling, also came round the table. I unrolled the two large photographs and they were silent at once. About one-and-a-half hours later, as we were going, Mr Lee apologised to me for their amused welcome. 'After your phone call I said to them all, "We've got a first class crank coming to see us on Friday and you can take an hour off to meet him."' It was raining, so he gave me a seven-foot plastic bag for my photographs which were mounted on board. Naturally he had plenty of plastic bags that size!

When they had taken an all-over look at both photographs I pointed out the scorches from the fire, the backs and fronts of the body, the scourging, the wounds, and Vignon's theory of how the stains had been formed. Then they started pointing out small details to each other.

After a time I said, 'What about the chest wound?'

'That would have done little damage. Put your hand where the point entered as on the Shroud photograph, and then lift your arms to the side in the crucifixion position, and it was too high to damage anything if the wound came from below. It would have bled, as we can see, and it might have allowed water between the lung and its cavity to come out at the same time. That water, the pleural effusion, would have been formed when the body was scourged. The lung would have been forced back, but even if the weapon had entered the lungs they can localise the injury.'

Then I asked, if the chest wound could not have been fatal, what did the man die of?

For perhaps thirty minutes they discussed this before I had a consensus report. It was this: 'If he lived before the seventeenth century, he would have been dead. He may have been unconscious on the cross and barely breathing, so he would have been dead to the onlookers. That's what they looked for. After Harvey they would have tested his pulse which would have been beating weakly. If he had lived in the twentieth century he would have been certified as in a coma.'

When discussing death we must be clear which standards we use for judging it. Different criteria are applied as medical knowledge improves. Many certified as dead not long ago would be considered just alive now and attempts made, with new methods, to revive them. Comparatively recently, in late Victorian times, the recovery of life by those thought dead was sufficiently frequent for many to leave instructions in their wills for their death to be checked, for instance by cutting off fingers or toes. As late as 1887 a design was patented for the 'saving of buried persons'. It consisted of an airline from the coffin so that anyone recovering consciousness could raise the alarm. Another had a line going up a tube to the surface attached to a suspended bell. That was a century ago, but even these days newspapers occasionally report cases of people recovering after having been certified dead, some after a considerable time.

Our current standards will no longer apply in future. Some Americans are apparently having their bodies deep-frozen on death in the hope that future technology will be able to revive them, to enjoy life again like Rip Van Winkle. Should this happen, those revived in this way cannot blame us for having pronounced them dead now. In the same way recoveries of life in former times are recorded frequently enough for us to assume they were far more frequent than they are now.

The forensic scientists argued that the body in the Shroud was *absolutely dead by pre-seventeenth century standards* but in a deep coma by present-day ones.

The grounds for their deductions were these. Any chemical staining reaction, whether ammonia-aloes or the action of some other agent on linen, would almost certainly have depended on temperature: the higher the temperature the darker the stain. For simple reactions a rule-of-thumb rule is that the rate of reaction doubles for every rise in temperature of ten Centigrade degrees. Photographers are aware of how a slightly higher temperature means that a film develops to the correct darkness in a shorter time, and cooks find that the few degrees' higher cooking temperature obtained with a pressure cooker means that the time required is considerably less. The depth of staining over the length of the front and back of the body is fairly constant, so the temperature of the cloth must also have been approximately uniform. This could only happen if the blood were still circulating, the heart just beating. The body must have been in a coma, therefore, and not clinically dead by twentieth-century standards.

As soon as a body dies, its heart stops beating, and the blood is no longer forced round the body keeping the temperature nearly even. Very soon the extremities—feet, hands, nose—which have a large surface area compared with the matter they hold, cool down to the outside temperature. The trunk of the body and the head hold a very great deal of heat and will retain this for many hours. Not only that, but the blood, no longer kept circulating, will naturally fall through gravity, causing lividity on the bottom surface. Some of these places, the buttocks and shoulder-blades in a prone body, for instance, would therefore stay warm even longer, so that the signs of that warmth should have been visible as darker areas on the Shroud. Had it covered a dead body, the forensic experts would have expected no stain at all towards the feet, and the hands and nose would also have shown much less stain than they do. At the University of Leeds Department of Forensic Medicine they have videotaped bodies as they cool after death with thermographic cameras, and these effects can be seen clearly.[3] The difference between the temperature of the surfaces of a corpse and the rectal temperature is the prime method a forensic scientist has for estimating how long it has been dead.

' In view of the fact that men get cold hands, feet and nose when they go out in cold weather, in spite of the circulation of their blood, it seems surprising that the man in the Shroud, in a state of coma with his heart only just beating, experienced so little change in temperature along the length of his body.

Unfortunately there are obvious reasons why scientific experiments with people's bodies in a state of coma are not easy to arrange, at any rate for someone not in the medical profession. Nor is it easy to find scientific papers that have investigated surface temperatures of live bodies. There is one that concerns experiments carried out in the New York Hospital in 1938. This found that the temperature along the body kept reasonably constant until the outside temperature fell more than five degrees Centigrade below the body temperature, when the temperature of the feet fell rapidly with the drop in temperature.[4] However, the people in the experiment were naked, and so they would have lost heat more rapidly, particularly as the skin would have evaporated freely. Under a cloth there would not have been this type of loss to any extent, and the cloth would also have cut down loss by convection and conduction, while radiation energy would have been partly reflected back. In view of the much lower rate of metabolism, the temperature could possibly have remained reasonably constant, provided the outside temperature in the tomb (assuming the body lay in the Shroud in a tomb) was not very low. On Easter Day 1981 a thermometer placed on the burial ledge in the Garden Tomb in Jerusalem at sunset read 22°C, a few degrees below a comatose body.

To see if the effect of a live body on a cloth covering it could be demonstrated, I obtained a linen sheet from the Lambeg Industrial Research Association of Northern Ireland, as near as possible to the published characteristics of the Shroud. The drama studio where I worked seemed the most suitable place for the experiment, but I was worried that the draughts might lessen the possibility of obtaining a sharp image. The cold was another factor, as the volunteer's toes and hands might lose temperature. A mattress was placed on the floor, and a volunteer lay on it, breathing through a length of Bunsen burner tubing so that his breath would not warm the cloth all round his head. The sheet was placed on him for four minutes. After that time it was raised to the vertical, viewed both by a thermographic camera connected to the television monitor and videotape recorder, and by a 35mm camera. As recorded by the thermographic camera, the body was quite clear on the sheet, the image going the whole length of the body. Lack of sharpness was due as much to the thermographic camera as to the draughts (see plates 19 and 20).

This evidence from the forensic scientists, that the body in the Shroud was in a coma rather than absolutely dead by twentieth-century standards, could remove the barriers to Vignon's vaporographic theory. There were two main problems. Firstly, since the gas would have been of a uniform density all round the body under the cloth, there would have been a large area of general stain, with none of the gradation seen on the Shroud. The second problem was the existence of the stains on only the closest fibres, for the gas would have affected the cloth as it diffused through.

If the skin temperature is assumed to have been a constant, but, since the body was in a comatose state, higher than the temperature outside the cloth, both points could be explained. The temperature of the cloth at any point would depend on how close it was to the skin. Where it was in contact it would have been skin temperature; as it moved away it would get cooler until, beyond a certain distance, it would have been more or less the same as the outside temperature. It follows that the closer the cloth to the skin, the higher the tempera- ture. And, since the staining process was almost certain to have depended on the temperature, *the closer the cloth to the skin, the darker the stain*; this is the three-dimensional information characteristic no other theory has managed to explain.

The second problem with the vaporographic theory may be answered bearing in mind the very low conductivity of still air. Air is an excellent insulator of heat provided it is kept still, which explains why people wear light, fluffy clothes that trap the air in their fibres, and put foam in the cavities in house walls. When the sheet was placed on top of the body, convection and radiation between the skin and the cloth carried heat much more than conduction, so that although there was a temperature gradient across the air gap—which explains why the greater the gap, the greater the difference in temperature—the temperature dropped much more rapidly at the surface of the linen.

The STURP team reported linen fibrils that were stained at one end and not at the other. There is no surprise in that either. Physics teachers can enliven their lessons with quite a few spectacular demonstrations—spectacular because they are surprising. One of these is to boil water in a paper con- tainer—a schoolchild's 'water-bomb' does admirably, par- ticularly if you make it with wings to hold it by—on the flame of a Bunsen burner. Provided there is water inside, the paper shows no sign of scorching, even though it is held right down on the flame. It is an admirable demonstration of the insulat- ing property of still air, for it is the air trapped in the fibrils of the paper pointing down into the flame that takes the enor- mous temperature gradient between the flame and the paper- water mass. If you have never seen the experiment and do not think it works, try it. The way in which a fibril on the Shroud, pointing down towards the body, was differentially stained along its length, should be clear.

The skin temperature may not have been constant every- where. The bruises from scourging can be seen clearly all over the back and legs of the dorsal image of the Shroud, but they are not blood-marks but body-marks. If no blood was circulating in the body there is no apparent reason for the staining being darker on those places. With the body in a coma, there might well have been a slight increase in temperature on the bruises as the blood flowed through the damaged blood vessels.

Quantitative information on the variation in skin temperature is difficult to obtain, but an enquiry to the Thermographic Unit of St Bartholomew's Hospital in London, where thermographic studies of sports and similar injuries are conducted, produced the following facts from Dr Cooke and Mr Mark Tooley:

a If the injury is not deep, immediately after the injury up to a variable period afterwards (perhaps 1–2 weeks) there is increased heat around the wound.

b Inflammation usually causes local heating.

c Increases are of the order of 1–2 degrees Centigrade.

That very slight increase in temperature where the cloth was pressed against the bruises by the sand on which the body rested might well explain the stains on the back showing on the otherwise nearly uniform tone.

Members of the STURP team rejected Vignon's theory for the two reasons now explained. However, they were also unhappy at not being able to find any traces of the chemicals they thought would have remained in the cloth as a result of the ammonia-aloes reaction. Nevertheless, they did report that they managed to obtain stains most nearly like the body-marks on the cloth by baking some linen which had a coating of perspiration, myrrh and aloes!

They may have been right: Vignon was possibly incorrect in suggesting that particular reaction. That does not necessarily affect the issue. Suppose later experiments show that the presence of some other agent throughout the cloth caused the stains during the time it wrapped the man's body. The rate at which that agent worked, whatever it was, would have depended on the temperature at any point. Vignon's argument was perfectly correct in saying that the gas between the skin and the cloth must have caused the stain since the skin acted over a distance; but the gas could have been warm air! It was the air that carried the heat upwards and raised the temperature of the cloth, so that the stains seen there represent a temperature map.

The man in the Shroud must have been in a coma, therefore, and not dead. The main evidence for this is twofold: the evenness of the stains along the length of his body (see plate 7), and the three-dimensional information. The question arises: what happened to him then?

He could have died completely, or he could have come round again within a reasonable time. If he died, his body must have been removed from the cloth shortly afterwards, for decomposition would have destroyed both the cloth and the stains. Decomposition starts remarkably rapidly in the part of the world where the cloth was made, and because of this burial must take place by law within twenty-four hours.

There is also the possibility that he recovered, his metabolic rate and temperature climbing up again to the normal and consciousness returning. However, this seems hardly likely when the stains showed that he was cruelly scourged and then crucified. It depends on what precisely was involved in the process of crucifixion.

8

Crucifixion

Descriptions exist of crucified men being taken down from the cross and surviving. One is given by the Jewish historian Josephus, who changed sides and joined the Roman army. He includes this passage in his autobiography:

And when I was sent by Titus Caesar with Caerealius and a thousand horsemen to a certain village called Thecoa, in order to know whether it were a place fit for a camp, as I came back I saw many captives crucified and remembered three of them as my former acquaintances. I was very sorry at this in my mind, and went with tears in my eyes to Titus and told him of them; so he immediately commanded them to be taken down and to have the greatest care taken of them in order to bring about their recovery; yet two of them died under the physician's hands, while the third recovered. [IV:75]

It is not clear how long the survivor spent on the cross, but a considerable time is implied. The time factor is very important.

One of the main investigators of crucifixion and the way in which the victims died was Dr Pierre Barbet, a French surgeon and anatomist. From the publication of Enrie's photographs in 1931 onwards, he made a close study of the wounds on the Shroud, with particular emphasis on the details of crucifixion.

In his medical post he was able to experiment with cadavers, and this meant that where Vignon had reasoned, Barbet was able to perform practical experiments, sometimes with surprising results.

Considering the nail wound in the wrist first, Vignon had presumed that nails in the palms would not support a body on a plain cross. Barbet proved it using a dead body. Vignon pointed out that the nail had apparently been driven through the wrist, and realised that this would have given sufficient strength to hold the body. Barbet actually drove a nail through the wrist of an amputated arm. The wrist is a mass of bones, and it was not until he placed the nail against it, and struck hard with the hammer, that the nail forced its way through an unsuspected gap called 'The Space of Destot'. As the nail went through, it penetrated or displaced the long tendon coming from the forearm that flexes the thumb, which was drawn across the palm.[1] When he examined the Shroud and found that on neither hand was the thumb represented, he felt sure he had found the reason, and because any painter would have painted them in, he had discovered another potent indication that the stains were not forged. In fact the thumbs might also be missing because they were tucked under the opposite palms naturally, but the argument against the likelihood of the cloth being painted still holds.

The next question to be investigated was the exact cause of death. When the victim was raised on the cross, assuming it was the normal sort, the plain *crux immissa* seen on Christian altars, his body would have sagged and his weight been borne on his arms. Barbet fastened volunteers on crosses, binding their hands and feet to the wood, to observe what happened. Each volunteer found that his chest was kept fully expanded when his weight was borne by his arms, with no possibility of exhaling. In this position he was slowly suffocated, and cramps which began in the arms spread to the trunk and legs. Because he could not breathe out and then in, the oxygen in his blood decreased and he would have asphyxiated in a matter of minutes. The only way the volunteer could stay alive was to press up with his feet, lessening the strain on his hands and arms, and breathing out and in rapidly until he had to collapse again through exhaustion. Eventually, and after a fairly short time, tiredness prevented the volunteer from pressing up on his feet, and he would have died from asphyxiation if not released.[2]

Barbet used the two positions to explain the V-shaped blood-marks on the left wrist. Although emerging from one wound, there are two quite separate streams of blood. Using pencil and paper instead of a live body, Barbet sketched the angles of the arms in the two positions, the one when all the weight was on the arms and the one when the feet had pressed the body up to allow breathing out and in. Measuring the two angles made by the V-shaped blood-marks with the line of the forearm, he constructed theoretically the two positions of the body so that those lines would have been vertical in the two positions. It seemed very plausible, and has apparently remained unquestioned until now.

There is one obvious problem with this idea. The victim must have switched from one position to the other quite frequently, so that the branches of the bloodstains would not have been distinct lines. There would at least have been a zigzagging between the two directions. To have them separate, the arm must have been in one position for some time while the blood slowly ran down to the end of the first trickle, and then for a similar period in the second position.

The question of time is vital. It must have been extremely difficult, with the feet nailed against the vertical beam, and the knees bent, to press up sufficiently to exhale once or twice, and to hold that position must have been very painful. So little breathing would have been possible that it is difficult to imagine a victim could have stayed alive for more than a few minutes.

There are few ancient records of crucifixion, but those that do exist indicate how long it took for the unfortunate victims to die. It was certainly not quick. The slowness was part of the torture, as well as the humiliation, hunger, thirst and exhaustion. Passers-by were meant to learn from the examples made of the victims, which is why crucifixions took place outside city walls and beside main roads. After defeating Spartacus, Crassus had six thousand prisoners nailed to crosses beside the Via Appia between Capua and Rome,[3] and Titus had up to five hundred prisoners a day nailed up on crosses outside the walls of Jerusalem, hoping that the gruesome sight of countless crosses would persuade the besieged to surrender.[4] As for the slowness of the death, Seneca, in Epistle 101 to Lucilius, writes that a lengthy process of dying is no longer worthy of the name of 'life', and follows it with a description of the gradual death of a victim of crucifixion:

> Can anyone be found who would prefer wasting away in pain dying limb by limb, or letting out his life drop by drop, rather than expiring once for all? Can any man be found willing to be fastened to the accursed tree, long sickly, already deformed, swelling with ugly weals on shoulders and chest, and drawing the breath of life amid long-drawn-out agony? He would have many excuses for dying even before mounting the cross.[5]

The *New Bible Dictionary* says of crucifixion: 'Death by this method was usually quite protracted, rarely supervening before thirty-six hours, and on occasion taking as long as nine days.'[6]

Ancient Jewish writings also indicate that death by crucifixion took a long time. The rabbis, in the Mishna, entered into long discussions as to how death was defined; it was not sufficient merely to see a man crucified on a cross, unless animals had eaten his body. In the Jerusalem Talmud, they point out that a rich lady might redeem a victim's body, the implication being that rich ladies would bribe officials to take down the sufferers and that in some cases at least they recovered. The rabbis also accepted that a man being crucified could authorise a bystander to issue a bill of divorcement to his wife, so that crucifixion victims were clearly regarded as being of sound enough mind to be able to conduct legal business.

These accounts do not fit in with the very brief, excruciating agonies suggested by the experiments of Barbet. Similar research was conducted by Dr Hermann Moedder, a German radiologist. He experimented by tying up on plain crosses university students – volunteers of course! He found that they fainted after six to twelve minutes because their blood pressure dropped, and that death would have followed in under half-an-hour. Again, there was no question of being sane enough to carry out legal business from the cross, and death would have come much earlier than records suggest. However, Moedder found that if the legs were supported every three minutes, normal circulation returned. He concluded that if the victim had had a footrest, he could have survived for hours, even days.[7]

His reason for choosing a footrest to stand on instead of the *sedile*, or type of saddle, of historical records to sit on was the fact that the way of finally despatching victims was to break their legs. He reasoned that this act would not have killed them had they been sitting on a *sedile*. That is true. However, they were possibly tipped forward off their supports when the time came to finish them off, and their legs would have been broken to prevent them from pressing themselves up onto their seats again.

A useful reference book on crucifixion is called exactly that, *Crucifixion*, in the English translation. It is by Martin Hengel, and in the original German had the lengthy title, *Mors turpissima crucis: Die Kruezigung in der antiken Weld und die 'Torheit' des 'Wortes vom Kreux'*. Hengel outlines the wide variety of practice, summarising it thus:

> Even in the Roman empire, where there might be said to be some kind of 'norm' for the course of the execution (it included a flogging beforehand, and the victim often carried the beam to the place of execution, where he was nailed to it with outstretched arms, raised up and seated on a small wooden peg), the form of execution could vary considerably: crucifixion was a punishment in which the caprice and sadism of the executioners were given full rein.

From this it is clear that, although there was wide variation, the normal support for the victim was not a footrest, the support represented in medieval paintings and used by Dr Moedder, but the projecting peg, the *sedile*, astride which the victim usually sat. Seneca, in his *Epistolae*, speaks of sitting on the cross, and implies that the projection had a sharp edge for the additional discomfort of the sufferer. St Justin describes the peg as 'this wood of the cross which is fixed in the middle, which sticks upwards like a horn, on which those who are crucified are seated'. St Irenaeus says that the cross had five extremities; it was on the fifth that the crucified man rested.

The alternative support for prolonging the agony was the *suppedaneum*, a horizontal bracket coming out from the upright, to which the feet were nailed. Although the foot-rest was always selected as the support when artists began painting crucifixion scenes, the first references to it in writings do not appear until much later than the *sedile*; not until the sixth century, in fact, in *De Gloria Martyrii* by Gregory of Tours.[8]

It is worth studying the stains on the cloth to see whether there is an indication which kind of support, if any, the man in the Shroud had. It is highly likely that he had one, if he did not die but slipped into a coma.

The most indicative stains are the blood-marks on the wrist and forearms. On the left wrist, the only one visible, are the V-shaped blood-marks, at an angle to the arm, while farther up the left forearm most of the marks are approximately parallel to one branch of the V. On the right forearm the blood-marks run parallel to the forearm, the right wrist being hidden. They are quite different from the left arm, and the right forearm must have been vertical a long time for the blood to trickle all the way down it from the wound on the wrist (see plates 21 and 22).

I carried out an experiment at Trent Polytechnic to investigate the significance of these marks. Blood-marks similar to the ones on the Shroud were painted on a volunteer's wrists and arms. This was done by projecting a slide on him while matching red marks were applied. A cross was then constructed with scaffolding in the drama studio. Hanging from the cross-beam with his hands equidistant from the vertical, facing the cross so that the blood-marks could be seen, the volunteer tried to pull himself up with his right forearm vertical so that the blood could have flowed down it through gravity. His left arm was nearly horizontal then, and his right biceps were under a very great strain, since his right arm was supporting almost his entire weight. It seemed entirely unrealistic that the crucified man would have pulled himself up to this extraordinary, asymmetric position to exhale, especially considering the force on his right nail-wound, and he could not possibly have held it while the blood slowly trickled down his arm.

Next, a short projection of wood was attached to the upright for him to sit on. The volunteer insisted that a small cushion should be put on it. The height was simply adjusted so that he could sit on it symmetrically, the marks across the left forearm and one limb of the V on his left wrist being vertical. This would have been the normal position when conscious. He was then asked to relax, as if losing consciousness, and topple to the right. Not only were the stains on his right forearm then vertical, but the second arm of the V was as well. He also found this position natural and comfortable (see plates 23 and 24).

The blood on the right arm issued from the wrist wound, but what caused the blood trickles coming from points on his left? They flow across the arm only. What could have caused those sharp wounds in the man's arm shortly before he fell to the right, unconscious?

The chest wound provides additional evidence that there must have been a *sedile*. A sharp instrument pierced the chest just under the right armpit, higher than in the position in the Shroud, for the skin would have moved as the arm was raised. If his body had been symmetrical when this wound was made, the blood would have dripped down his stomach and right leg and the marks of it would have been visible along the cloth. This is not the case, and no blood can be seen below the chest. If the man was stabbed in the unconscious position on the *sedile*, the blood would have flowed down his side and so would not have been shown on the cloth. When he was placed in the cloth after being brought down to the ground, the blood flow round his back on the dorsal image was clearly much more watery than the other blood-marks.

This is not surprising. When he was scourged, he would probably have had a pleural effusion, a watery liquid between his lungs and his rib-cage. Collapsed unconscious to the right, this would have been drained when the chest was pierced, so that watery liquid as well as blood would have come out.

There is one more deduction we may make from the blood-stains. The stains are perfectly clear. Had he been nailed with his back to the wood the marks would have been completely smudged by the wood. The same applies to the feet, which are clear enough to suggest they were not against the wood or against each other. He must have faced the cross.

In this case, how could the feet have been nailed together onto the wood? The ankle of the first would have prevented the second being close enough on top of it to have the same nail driven through. Again the bloodstains suggest the answer. The feet were nailed separately. The left leg was bent sharply and the foot nailed first. Note that the blood flows across his left sole. That bend of the knee is recorded, in a small way, on the Shroud where the left leg looks slightly shorter. The right foot was clearly below, with the flows along the foot. The blood at the back of the heel may have been drips from the foot above.

With the man facing the wood, the cross could have been a simple T shape, and he could have seen over the top of it.

9

Detailed Observations

T he presence of a *sedile* on the cross of the man in the Shroud means that, in his case, all the research into how men died when crucified on plain crosses is irrelevant. It would have been possible for him to remain on the cross for a day or days, and then to fall into a coma before being taken down and placed in the cloth. The V-shaped blood-marks on his wrist suggest that he was suspended a consider-able time in the conscious position, and then a similar time slumped to the right while the blood trickled down the second arm of the V. His heart must have been beating throughout to keep up the blood pressure from the wound.

When the nail or nails were removed from his feet and he was taken down from the cross, blood flowed towards his heels from the nail-holes. This is not conclusive proof that his heart was still beating. When a dead body is moved, blood can flow out of wounds by gravity. However, the quantity of it under and beside his feet, and round his back, would suggest that he was still in a coma rather than dead.

There are some further details about the man to be learnt from the stains, and the fact that his body was placed in a long length of rich material also needs exploring (see plate 11).

Firstly, his stature. Clearly, looking at his image, he was well proportioned, and it might be presumed that close measure-ment of his physique would be possible. Unfortunately, precision is difficult on two counts: the edges of his body merge into the background, and the depth of the folding of the cloth into hollows has to be guessed. For these reasons the estimates of his height have varied between five foot four inches and six feet.[1] Measurements of the lengths of the images on the flat cloth have given 6.7257 feet for the front image and 6.8596 feet for the back,[2] although such accuracy is fanciful considering the blurred edges. The height most commonly estimated for the man is about five feet eleven inches, which would have been tall for the Mediterranean peoples, but not excessively so.[3]

Crucifixion itself had many forms, from a simple nailing to a stake to the man being fixed upside down on a cross shaped like an X. Sometimes the victim was alive, sometimes it was his dead body that was nailed up for display. From the Persians it spread among many barbarian races, and was taken over by the Romans, though not for Roman citizens. Constantine banned it throughout the Roman Empire in about AD 341,[4] so that one would assume the man in the cloth suffered his fate before that.

His looks are important, for the Romans and Greeks in the Empire shaved and dressed their hair, while the orthodox Jews left it to grow, except perhaps when mourning, wearing it at the back as a pigtail. The signs on the dorsal image of an unbound pigtail are also indicative.[5] So he was probably a Jew. Professor Carleton S. Coon is one of the world's most distinguished ethnologists, a former Harvard professor, and author of works on the racial characteristics of people all over the world. He has travelled widely, including the Middle East. His verdict was, 'He is of a physical type now found among Sephardic Jews and Arabs.'[6]

Because of this, irrespective of when the crucifixion may have taken place, references will be made to Jewish customs when discussing the Shroud and its marks. Many of the ways of the Middle Eastern Jews were similar to those of the Arabs of that area in recent times.

The stains give us some clues to the sort of environment the body was in when lying in the cloth. The image of the face seems unnaturally thin, and the cloth does not fall round the sides of the body as one would expect if it had been laid on a flat surface. Also, the back image folds up round the sides to give the same width as the front, which would not occur on a surface that was hard as well as flat. Paul Vignon, in considering the narrowness of the image of the face, pictured the cloth held up by cushions or similar supports at the sides of the head and holding up the hair. This seems credible, but supports would have been necessary all down the sides of the body as well, to keep the body and legs thin.

This does not adequately explain the back image. A more likely explanation of the top surface is that the space in which the body lay had a rim round it, so that the top of the cloth went directly from the body to the rim, keeping the top image narrow. The exact kind of space is uncertain, but either a trough or a sarcophagus would have given the right effect. It would have had to be about as tall as the height of a prone body, perhaps a foot, so that the cloth could have hung across its top edge. The width of the space could not have been much wider than the body, for the weight of the cloth would have dragged it back, so it can be thought of as being similar to a tight-fitting coffin. There is confirmatory evidence of this in the hands and arms. If a person lies on the floor and folds his hands in the 'fig-leaf' position as in the Shroud, he finds that if he goes limp his elbows will fall to the ground and his hands come apart. So the elbows must have been prevented from falling to the sides of the body by the constraints of the space, the sides of the trough or coffin.

This still does not answer the problem of the width of the back image. The cloth is only 110 cms (43 inches) wide. If the middle 51 cms (20 inches) pressed against the back, this would have left less than 30 cms on either side, too little to stretch up to be supported on the rim. The edges of the cloth must therefore have lain along the edges of the body. Some other explanation is required for the broad image of the back. On the VP-8 Image Analyser the man's back had no subtle slopes but appeared uniformly flat, as if the skin had been evenly in contact with the cloth over the whole area. This could not happen with a hard surface.

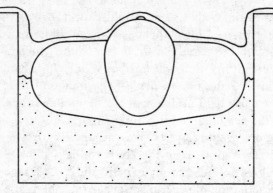

5   *Cross-section of the body lying on sand in the tomb, with the cloth lightly covering it.*

The answer is probably that the body rested on sand. This was normal practice in areas of the Middle East, and is mentioned in the Mishna.[7] The cross-section of the body and the cloth in the open coffin or trough would have been as shown in the diagram above.

Note that the arms would have been kept well above the sand, and this would be confirmed if no arms appeared on the dorsal image on the cloth. Unfortunately, these crucial areas are obscured by the broadest scorch stains and the widest patches on the whole Shroud.

Some other points can be deduced by applying to particular areas the thermographic hypothesis, in which the darkness of the body-stains depends on the temperature of the cloth. The surprising darkness round the nose can be explained by the minimal exhaling of warm breath. The nose projects so far from the face that the cloth must have been held away from the skin all around it; but the moustache and beard are stained, as well as the skin on the sides of the face.

When considering the temperature of the cloth, the darkness of the hair, as well as that of the beard and moustache, is difficult to understand. They would have been considerably colder than the body. Perhaps it is because there are two factors to the darkness of the stain: the temperature of the cloth at that point and the concentration of the developing agent. The developing agent—ammonia, if Vignon was correct—could have been much more prevalent in the hair than on the surface of the skin. But this is no more than a guess.

The darkness of the stains underneath the feet indicates, as Vignon surmised, that there must have been material underneath the feet pressing the bottom of the cloth against the soles. The stains all the way down the backs of the legs show that the knees were not bent much, the left being only slightly raised, so the soles must have come up at a considerable angle to the horizontal, and the cloth would not have touched them at all unless it was pressed against them by a pile of material.

At the other end of the body, the blood-marks and body-marks all round the back of the hair show that there must have been material around and under the head as well, in the form of a pillow. This is more likely than simply rolls of material by the side of the head, as Vignon suggested, for two reasons. Firstly, all round the back of the head was in contact with the cloth. Secondly, there is evidence that the head was pressed up: the back of the neck looks as if it was stretched, and the dorsal image on the Shroud is longer than the frontal (see plate 25).[8]

Little more has been deduced about the man, his ordeal, and his position when in the cloth. However, we need to consider how he came to be placed, naked and unwashed, in an expensive length of cloth, for a considerable time. Customs and beliefs matter in this respect.

If the man was a Jew, to his fellow Jews his body would have been considered cursed. In Deuteronomy (21:23), part of the Torah or sacred Mosaic Law, it says quite specifically that 'he that is hanged (upon the tree) is accursed of God'. *Any* dead body was considered polluting to the touch,[9] and this rule would have applied much more strongly to someone dying in this way.

This is why the rich cloth, and the body placed in it somewhere with a steady temperature, like a tomb or cellar, come as a surprise. In Roman times guards would have been responsible for the bodies of those crucified. Often the dead victims were left up for animals to devour. Many were thrown into a communal grave or lime-pit. Compared with normal treatment, the body of the man in the cloth was treated with remarkable respect, but at the same time, for some reason he was not given the proper burial rites.

It is not possible to be certain about Jewish burial customs as long ago as the times when crucifixions were carried out, but there are probabilities that can be deduced from studying the few descriptions preserved in the Rabbinic literature. Firstly, the eyes were closed, and the chin may have been bound up at this stage.[10] The corpse was then washed with warm, perfumed water and anointed with an unguent perhaps consisting mainly of salt, honey, myrrh and cedar oil,[11] but it is not known whether the anointing was done by pouring a fluid on the body, sprinkling the clothes before putting them on, rubbing the body or immersing it. Next, it was clothed in its burial garments. It was thought a dishonour for a corpse to be naked, and grave-clothes became finer and more expensive as time went on—so much so that dying people were often abandoned by their relatives so that the community would be responsible for the expense of the funeral.[12] At last Rabbi Gamaliel, who died in AD 57–58, directed that he should be buried in the simplest of linen garments, and his example was eagerly followed. Whatever clothes were put on the body, the face was left uncovered. The hands and feet were probably bound, and the jaw tied up with a band.

There was probably one exception to this rule of washing and anointing corpses, although the Jewish literature describing it—the sixteenth-century *Code of Jewish Law*—dates from well after the time when the Romans banned crucifixion and the period indicated by carbon-dating. Blood was considered so important to the Jews that if a man died a violent death and his blood was spilt onto his clothes, they were not removed and he was buried unwashed. This could possibly have applied to the man in the Shroud. However, he was naked, and although he would not have been washed because of the blood on his skin, completely wrapping him so that his face as well as his body was covered seems surprising. The face had to be left uncovered. It is possible that the use of the Shroud instead of the usual burial garments implies a hurried and provisional covering of the body.

The reason for the anointing, and for placing the body on sand, was to put off the beginning of corruption for as long as possible—three days at least. The Jews and many other races believed that the soul remained with the body for three days after death and might re-enter it during that period, allowing the body to come alive again. The period of mourning was seven days, but for the first three days relatives kept visiting the tomb in case the body recovered from death. During this period the tomb was not properly closed. Families sometimes hired men to watch by the dead for them.[13]

The existence of these beliefs suggests that mistakes were commonly made, bodies being interred in what is now known as a deep coma. In view of the means by which death was recognised then, this is not surprising. Until a few centuries ago, it was thought that life resided as breath in the chest; when a body showed no signs of breathing, particularly if the chest was wounded, it was declared dead. The Greek word *pneuma* could mean breath or life, spirit or ghost, so the phrase 'he gave up the ghost' or 'he yielded up his spirit' could be just as well translated 'he stopped breathing'. The function of the heart and the circulation of the blood were not discovered for more than a millennium and a half. Even today, with all our sophisticated medical knowledge, people recover after being declared clinically dead, sometimes in the mortuary.

It may be argued that the Romans, being experienced in killing by crucifixion, could not possibly have made a mistake and allowed the body of someone who was only comatose to be taken away. The Roman centurion in charge had the duty, as *exactor mortis*, of confirming death in the victims. The answer is that the man in the cloth was absolutely dead by the centurion's standards and experience. If men before him, after choking on offered wine, for instance, had slumped to the side in what is now known as a coma, they would not have survived, for being dumped in a lime-pit or communal grave would have given no chance of recovery. The centurion would not have known that full life could return from such a condition.

*   *   *

Up to this point the book has been a brief survey showing how far the study of the cloth and its stains, and the relevant historical sources, can take us at the present time.

Many of the questions raised have not been answered: questions such as who the man was; why the crucifixion took place and where; and why the crucified man was placed, naked and unwashed, in a rich length of cloth. What happened to his body then? And what could have caused those strange blood-marks in the skin round the top of his head? We might guess there was a crown of thorns on top of his head. The only recorded instance in history of such a punishment being used was in the crucifixion of Jesus Christ. So if the man in the Shroud *was* crucified in the period suggested by carbon-dating, he must for some reason have been given the same torture as Jesus.

10

Can It Have Been Forged?

Before considering this in detail it is worth summarising what has been revealed by our study of the cloth:

1 The large twill piece of cloth, 4.35m by 1.1m (14′3″ by 3′7″), is a good quality three-to-one twill weave in pure linen, with only the odd traces of cotton as impurities. Its dimensions equal 8 × 2 Assyrian cubits. These were used in commerce in the Middle East not long before and after the year 0.

2 The evidence of impurities in the fabric, and of pollen on its surface, indicates manufacture in the Middle East—Syria or Palestine rather than Egypt—and most of its time spent there in the open air or exposed to air from open windows.

3 The date of manufacture is uncertain. The technology for weaving three-to-one twill existed three or four thousand years ago, but equivalent *linen* cloths did not appear regularly until the end of the Middle Ages, although that may be because only the funerary linen cloths were preserved.

4 Very dim stains and patches can be seen on the cloth. The main marks were the result of damage from a fire in 1532.

5 Between the scorch marks can be seen the faint images of the front and back of a man's body, and the face suggests someone of Middle Eastern origin.

6 These images could not have been painted, nor could they

have been forged by any other known method without the use of a live man's body.

7 The man has wounds from scourging, crucifixion and a stab-wound in the chest. He also has blood-marks from where the skin round the top of his head was punctured.

8 The blood-marks were caused by human blood, probably of group AB. The formation of the body-stains is not yet understood.

9 He was crucified on a cross with a *sedile* on which he sat upright for some hours. He then toppled to the right, presumably on losing consciousness, to remain in that second position for a similarly long time.

10 While toppled to the right, he was stabbed in the right side of his chest, just below the armpit. The watery trickle of blood from the wound suggests that he was suffering from a pleural effusion as a result of being scourged.

11 He was still in a coma when he was placed in the cloth and must have remained in it for a long time while the stains developed.

12 His body was in the cloth in an open coffin or trough-shaped space, in the bottom of which was sand. Some soft material was under his shrouded head, pillowing it, while another pile of material was beneath his feet, holding the cloth against his soles.

13 His body was not prepared for burial. It was unwashed and not anointed, and was naked under the cloth. His head was covered.

14 As he was in a deep coma, although absolutely dead by contemporary standards, he could have recovered at any time within a few days, or died.

15 His body left the cloth alive or newly dead, since decay did not affect the image.

So how could it have come about? With the carbon-dating result of 1260–1390, the Shroud in Europe by 1357, and the majority of its time in the open in the area round Jerusalem, it must have happened near the older limit of 1260.

The ninth and last crusade in 1270 failed when Louis IX and a large part of his army died at Tunis. The Kingdom of Acre was the last Christian outpost, with the ports of Acre, Tyre, Sidon and Beirut. They were surrounded by the empire of the Mamelukes. In 1291 Tyre, Sidon and Beirut were evacuated and the last Christian stronghold was overcome. The castle was under siege for 53 days by an army of tens of thousands who used big catapults to lob bombs into the fortress, and 1,000 miners burrowed a bastion to lay a large charge of dynamite and bring it down. The captured knights and foot-soldiers became slaves, and the girls were sent to the Damascus slave-market where they were said to be so plentiful that a girl could be bought for a single drachma.

Among the captured soldiers, it has been suggested, was the man in the Shroud. Just as the Japanese mocked the Christianity of their prisoners-of-war by crucifying a few of the British and Australians they held, so the triumphant Arabs crucified one of the soldiers and afterwards laid his body carefully in a long piece of cloth.

That seems to be the most plausible explanation anyone has offered yet, and the matter seems to be resting there.

However, there are big flaws in that theory:

1 It is difficult to believe that Arabs would have mocked Christianity and Christians in that way when the Arabs regard Jesus as a very great prophet second only to Mahomet. If that is not sufficient argument:

2 Even if they did so, they would probably have simply nailed the prisoner to a cross of wood.

3 The method of Roman crucifixion was lost after the official ban in the fourth century, so they would not have used a cross with a *sedile* which we know from study of ancient literature was normally used, nor would they have nailed their victim through the wrists instead of the palms.

4 The detail with which Jesus' Crucifixion was reconstructed

is incredible. Consider the scourging with a Roman *flagrum*, the buffeting, the crown of thorns. Consider the spear thrust after hours on the Cross, sufficient to let out the pleural effusion and some blood to agree with the 'water and blood' description in St John's Gospel. Then again, the body fell into a coma for no apparent reason and was then left on the cross for a further few hours. Consider the removal of the body, wrapping it in very rich cloth coated with the funerary herbs before laying it in an enclosed place with a constant temperature—probably a tomb—long enough for the stains to develop. Consider then the recovery of the man, and the keeping of the cloth secretly in air so that it could gather many seasons' worth of pollen. As the Christians had left for good by then, how could it have reached Geoffrey de Charny? Incidentally, a large face, similar to the Mandylion and reckoned to be an idol of the defending knights, was found in the fortress of Acre by the Arabs after the defeated forces had left.

5 They would not have used a stretch of very good quality twill, of the sort used for fine garments, and the coincidence of its measurements with the ancient 8 by 2 cubits is also remarkable.

 The artistic evidence, that the face in the Shroud had been the accepted face of Jesus since about the sixth century, must also be remembered.

Any possibility of the forging of the Shroud in the Middle Ages seems to be ruled out. The stains on the cloth must have been made earlier in that area, before the conquest by the Arabs, and probably before the banning of crucifixion throughout the Roman Empire. In which case the carbon-dating result is very seriously wrong. Is that at all possible?

11

Can Carbon-Dating
be Wrong?

S uppose that a baby called John is a very remarkable baby
because he has eaten one red sweet a day since birth.
You look at the wrapper beside his cot and see that it held
100 red sweets, and as there are just 22 left you can work out
that he must have eaten 78 red sweets, so must be 78 days
old.

Now suppose the packet of sweets holds red, green and blue
sweets but does not say how many sweets it held in the first
place. What it does say is that in the unopened packet there
is one red sweet in every six sweets. Therefore, if you add up
the green and blue and get 500, that means there were 100,
or 1/6th of 600, red sweets at the start. So if there are 22 left
John is 78 days old.

Carbon-dating is similar. It works by counting carbon
atoms instead of sweets. The carbon atoms in the Shroud are
of two sorts, stable and unstable. The vast majority are stable
and do not change—the green and blue sweets in John's
packet (C-12 and C-13 atoms). The red sweets, the radioactive
atoms (C-14), are slowly disappearing and becoming nitrogen.

The date we need for the Shroud is the year in which the flax
died, from which the linen of the Shroud was made. Up till that
time it was exchanging carbon with air and had the same proportion of stable and unstable carbons as the atmosphere.

The vast majority of the carbon atoms in the atmosphere are the two stable types. An extremely small proportion, about one in every trillion (1,000,000,000,000) instead of the 1 in 6 in the example, is radioactive carbon. That proportion is more or less constant. In the upper atmosphere nitrogen atoms are hit by cosmic rays and become radioactive carbon atoms, and at the same rate radioactive carbon atoms down below are decaying back into nitrogen atoms, so the proportion of radioactive carbon atoms in the atmosphere is almost constant.

The newly created radioactive carbon atoms in the upper atmosphere do not just float around as separate atoms but combine with oxygen atoms to become carbon dioxide, which sinks down to the earth and is breathed in by plants. That is why living creatures have, while alive, the same proportion of stable and unstable carbon atoms as the air has.

But they die. Absorption of carbon dioxide stops. The proportions of the carbon atoms are fixed at the moment of death in the same way as the proportions of the sweets in John's unopened packet. And just as John slowly ate the red sweets, the radioactive carbon atoms decay much more slowly into nitrogen.

In practice there is another complication, for the radioactive carbon does not decrease at a regular rate but at a rate depending on how many radioactive atoms are left. So the rate of decay decreases from the moment the plant dies. The formula for the change in the rate is known. After 60,000 years only one part in every 10^{15}, or 1,000,000,000,000,000, is radioactive carbon, and the accuracy of the apparatus for dating does not stretch more than half that time.

It follows that since scientists know the rate at which radioactive carbon atoms have decayed since the plant died, and can calculate from the stable carbon atoms how many radioactive atoms there were in the first place, they can work out the age of the sample.

In the 'old' gas counting method, the amount of carbon atoms is found by weighing to calculate the radioactive carbon atoms (and as the radioactive carbon was only one part in a trillion it makes very little difference), and the rate of decay is measured over a period of time. For instance, every time a radioactive atom disintegrated, a piece of apparatus could register that as a blip, so over a time the rate of disintegration could be calculated from the number of blips per hour. Knowing the original number of radioactive atoms and their rate of decay, the age of the specimen can be determined. To obtain a good result by that method about 25g is necessary to get a reasonable counter reading in a reasonably short time.

Recently another 'new' method, the AMS method used by the testing laboratories, has been devised (see plate 27). Just as light is split into its constituent colours by a prism, by firing all the molecules containing carbon atoms through a mass spectrograph the different carbon atoms are turned in separate circles according to their mass, the heavier ones turning a wider circle. Then the comparative amounts of the two stable carbon atoms and the radioactive atom can be worked out. The age can be calculated from these readings. The great advantage of the new method is that every radioactive carbon atom takes part in the reading and not merely those decaying to nitrogen over a given time. Approximately one-fifth the amount of material is required for this new method, and the 50g pieces given to the three laboratories were enough for them to carry out perhaps ten readings each. The old method might have obtained two readings.

Whichever method is used, pretreatment—getting rid of all accretions on the specimen so that only the original carbon remains—is essential, and in many ways this is the most important part of the experiment and the way mistakes most often arise. If some extra carbon has got into the specimen, the result is bound to be wrong.

The methods vary from one laboratory to another, but the principles are the same. When the samples are unpacked each is probably examined optically so that surface debris and dust is removed. Then it is vacuum cleaned. Ultrasonics may then be used to remove dust and pollen. An organic solvent may then be applied to get rid of any grease, and then it is dried and weighed. Next it probably has an acid wash followed by distilled water followed by an alkali wash also followed by distilled water. Lastly a bleach reduces it to its basic cellulose.

After drying and weighing it is probably sealed in a vacuum with copper oxide, and this is put in an oven at 950°C. It is burnt in the oxygen emitted by the copper oxide.[1]

In some laboratories the carbon dioxide is then put in an oven with zinc, with some iron powder to act as catalyst and binder. Zinc takes the oxygen from the carbon dioxide, and the carbon forms in the iron powder, and it is this mixture of pure carbon from the original specimen and the iron powder which is used in the Oxford apparatus.

It should be obvious from the minute proportion of radio-active carbon in the sample that the experiment has to be extremely exact, and to the layman it is quite extraordinary that such accuracy is possible. Can it be as foolproof a method of ageing as the public regard it?

Those who deal with carbon-dating results, the archaeologists, do not have such faith in it. The Biblical archaeologist Dr Eugenia Nitowski (now Carmelite nun Sister Damian of the Cross), said:

> In any form of inquiry or scientific discipline, it is the weight of evidence which must be considered conclusive. In archaeology, if there are ten lines of evidence, carbon-dating being one of them, and it conflicts with the other nine, there is little hesitation to throw out the carbon date as inaccurate due to unforeseen contamination.[2]

This is a view other archaeologists share. A specific case is reported by the highly respected Greek archaeologist Spyros Iakovidis:

> In relation to the reliability of carbon-dating, I would like to mention something which happened to me during my excavation at Gla (Boeotia, Greece). I sent to two different laboratories in two different parts of the world a certain amount of the same burnt grain. I got two

readings differing by 2,000 years, the archaeological date being right in the middle. I feel that this method is not exactly to be trusted.[3]

Condemnation indeed!

The laboratories concerned in experiments do not publish their wrong results. They would be unlikely to co-operate if asked what mistakes they had made. However, the results of famous cases are announced.

The two most widely publicised discoveries of bodies in recent years have been the Lindow Man and the Iceman of Hauslabjoch.

In 1984 the well-preserved body of an Iron Age man was found in the peat of Lindow Moss in Cheshire. Lindow Man officially, he became known as Pete Marsh. The date of the peat was found by the older method to be 300 BC. The gas-counting radiocarbon-dating laboratory at Harwell and the AMS laboratory at Oxford were used to date small samples of skin, and Oxford obtained AD 100 from its sample and Harwell AD 500. The differences remained even when the laboratories exchanged samples.[4] The British Museum labels the Lindow Man as 'lived and died between 300 BC and AD 100. Date in dispute'. They should have said between 300 BC and AD 500.

In September 1991 the frozen and wind-blown body of a young man was found in a high glacier on the Austro-Italian border. Archaeology confidently dated him to the beginning of the Bronze Age, about 2000 BC, from his flanged metal axe and other artefacts. The AMS carbon-dating laboratories in Oxford and Switzerland determined him to be from 3300 BC. Grasses associated with the man were dated by an Innsbruck laboratory to considerably younger than 3000 BC, but when Oxford and Zurich obtained the same result on a repeat experiment, the laboratory at Innsbruck conceded their results must have been 'wrongly published'. The archaeologists were upset by all this. They pointed out that although simple copper axes were known as far back as 2800 BC, those with flanges were thought to be considerably more recent. In a BBC television programme on the 'Iceman' a bemused archaeologist said that the radiocarbon-datings were 'designer-made to embarrass the prehistorians'. For some reason he did not qualify it by saying that the carbon-dating might be wrong.[5]

John Tyrer, a textile expert who has recently died, was an enthusiastic and respected member of the British Society for the Turin Shroud. From his knowledge of textiles he was convinced that the Shroud is far older than medieval. He was delighted, therefore, to be sent this cutting from the *Oxford Star* of 11 April 1991:

Red-faced boffins from Oxford University dropped a clanger when asked to date ancient rock-paintings by South African bushmen. Their carbon-dating tests estimated the rock to be 1,200 years old, but they were dumbfounded when grandma Joan Ahrens said she painted them just 11 years ago!

The rock shock started when a schoolboy in South Africa came across the paintings and his art teacher called in Natal Museum. They in turn sent the rock to Oxford University's AMS unit—which found the Turin Shroud was a fake—and their results confirmed the rocks were the first bushmen-painted rock.

Then 72-year-old Mrs Ahrens saw the articles and revealed she had painted them in art classes. They had been stolen by vandals and thrown into the bush.[6]

It is all very odd. If the carbon-dating results were correct, the old lady was using very ancient paints!

John Tyrer wrote to the local museum in Manchester, and asked if any mistakes had occurred in carbon-dating their exhibits. He was told in a letter:

In the case of Mummy 1770, which we unwrapped here in 1975, the carbon-dating produced different dates for the bones and the bandages of the mummy (the bones were approximately 800–1,000 years older than the bandages), which led us to speculate that the Mummy had been re-wrapped 800–1,000 years after its death. An alternative, of course, is that the resins and unguents used in mummification may affect the bandages and bone in ways that affect the carbon dates. This is one of the problems which we shall have to face in Egyptology in the near future. However, for our experience, carbon-dating of mummified remains and their associated bandages has produced some unexpected results.

'The resins and unguents used in mummification may affect the bandages and bone in ways that affect the carbon dates.' That could have applied to the Shroud.

In advising archaeologists how to pack materials sent for carbon-dating, Dr Bowman of the British Museum writes in her booklet *Radiocarbon Dating*:

Many materials used for preserving or conserving samples contain carbon that may be impossible to remove subsequently; do not use glues, biocides . . . (etc.). Many packing materials, such as paper, cardboard, cotton wool and string, contain carbon and are potential contaminants. Cigarette ash is also taboo.[7]

With the pretreatment used, it is extraordinary that such containers might have an effect.

Errors in carbon-dating results when dating ancient artefacts prompted comparative tests commissioned by the Science and Engineering Research Council in 1989. Thirty-eight laboratories round the world dated artefacts of known age. They were provided with samples made from wood, peat and carbonate. The laboratories involved were on average 'two to three times less accurate than implied by the range of error they stated.'

Murdoch Baxter, one of the organisers of the trial, pointed out that 'unaccounted-for sources of error occur during the processing and analysis of the samples.'

He reported that *accelerator mass spectrometry (AMS), the method used the previous year to date the Turin Shroud, came out of the survey badly.* Five of the 38 participants used this method and some of these laboratories were way out when dating samples as little as 200 years old. He reasoned that because so little material is used in AMS dating, the effects of chemical pre-treatment are likely to be more serious. 'The samples are more prone to atmospheric dust or dandruff,' he said.

Baxter suggested that the survey represented 'a major turning point in the history of the method'.[8]

Clearly the AMS method is often a considerable way out. What unusual factors in dating the Shroud would allow all three laboratories to get similar results a long way out?

12

The Shroud and the
Carbon-Dating

The carbon-dating of the Shroud was a very poor example of how a scientific experiment should be conducted. Apart from anything else, the laboratories concerned knew most of the answers they were expected to find before they had even started.

Various recommendations had been made by interested British and American groups. They had recommended that:

1 Both methods of carbon-dating should be employed.
2 Samples should be taken from several places on the Shroud. There are pieces behind the patches, for instance, which the Shroud could well lose without altering the cloth viewed.
3 Observers should be present throughout the sample-taking.
4 The tests should be conducted 'blind'.
5 Carbon-dating should be one of many experiments, some of them other methods of dating, so that the result of carbon-dating should not be seen as conclusive.

In the event none of this happened. As was described earlier, the newer AMS method was used exclusively; the decision of where to take the samples was not made until observers were there and then all came from one end; the cutting up of the samples and placing in metal canisters was done in a separate room away from cameras and observers; and as the experimenters had seen the Shroud they knew at once which sample belonged to it, and they were given the dates of the other samples.

There was a lot of criticism at the time, particularly from the laboratories not chosen. In the previous calibration test between seven laboratories, of which three were AMS, the one completely wild result had come from the AMS laboratory at Zurich. It was revealed later that when Professor Wölfli decided to test the Zurich apparatus with a piece of linen, he used a piece of the 50-year-old linen table-cloth which belonged to his mother-in-law. Carbon-dating measured it as 350 years old.[1]

However, looking at the results published in *Nature* on 16 February 1989, the three laboratories obtained remarkably similar results for the Shroud and the control samples.

Foul play has been suspected. Some think substitution took place during the half-hour when the samples were being weighed and packed in their containers. However, Michael Tite, who was one of the two involved in the unrecorded half-hour, is a respected scientist and he had no interest in obtaining any particular result.

Collusion between the three laboratories involved in the dating was forbidden, but although the heads of the laboratories may have kept their word, there is little doubt that the lesser scientists were in contact by telephone.

As for the results themselves, Remi van Haelst from Belgium carefully analysed the statistics published and spoke to scientists involved. He found out that Arizona had done eight measurements rather than four and they spanned 846 years, rather than the 445 published.[2]

In spite of all that, there is little doubt that the experiments did indeed find the age of the Shroud by carbon-dating to be 1260–1390, to a 95 per cent degree of certainty.

The first cause of error may have been the construction of the linen. At the Rome Conference on the Shroud in June 1993, two Russians, Dr Andrey A. Ivanov and Dr Dmitri Kouznetsov (who has been awarded the Lenin Prize), both of

Moscow's Laboratory of Physico-Chemical Research Methods, reported their researches on the structure of linen.

Firstly they studied how the linen was made. They found that as the flax grew, C-14 had a preference for the central fibres rather than the proteins, the waxes and fats, coating the plant. This effect was increased during the spinning process, and could lead to an enrichment of C-14 by as much as 40 per cent.

The second line of research studied linen heated to a very high temperature, approximately equal to that of the 1532 fire. Again they found there was addition to the radioactive content of the linen, partly due to evaporation of remaining proteins and lipids, and partly due to isotopic exchange. What this means is that when the linen is extremely hot the atoms can easily escape and exchange with similar atoms in the surrounding air, C-14 exchanging with C-12. The Russians calculated to show that the carbon-dating was out by 1,000 years approximately. This ties up with the dating of the Manchester Museum mummy: the shroud was dated to 1,000 years later than the body it wrapped.

The experiments are incomplete, but already Dr Van Oosterwyck-Gastuche, an instigator of this research, can say, 'I believe it is almost futile to try to calculate the true age of a textile as badly adulterated as the Shroud.'[3]

In that case, the cloth might well be at least 1,900 years old. Clearly the testing laboratories did not take these properties of linen into account. The research, which would mean the Shroud was genuinely of Christ's time, is at present being tested at other laboratories, and if proved correct will nullify the 1988 tests.

There are several other ways in which errors could have been introduced during the cloth's history. The Shroud did not stay put in a safe place like Pete Marsh or the Iceman. If it originates from the years when crucifixion was used as a punishment, it must have spent its early centuries somewhere unrecorded. It may have been in a place, for instance, where there was a spontaneous nuclear emission from the earth— one happened in Uganda not long ago—which would have increased its radioactive content. Nazri Iskander, Director of Conservation for the Egyptian Antiquities Department, and Dr Sayeed Mohamed Thebat, Faculty of Medicine at Cairo University, are at present investigating the chance discovery that mummies which rested on sand for centuries are radioactive, and they may find a way in which the cloth could have been affected. Ian Wilson, in his book *The Turin Shroud*, showed that a likely early history for the cloth included its being hidden within a wall at Edessa for more than five centuries up to AD 575. Radioactive material in the rocks could have affected the Shroud. *Considerably less than a 13 per cent increase in radioactive carbon during that time would have caused the results to be 1260–1390 instead of 33.*

Once on view to the public, probably in Constantinople after AD 1000, the Shroud would have picked up carbon in its fibres whenever it was handled or in a smoky atmosphere. People did not wear rubber gloves. Remarkably, even Riggi did not wear gloves when cutting off the strip in 1988! We know that in medieval times it was shown by the light of flaming torches. Candlewax was another contaminant, and it is always possible that someone tried to protect the image by applying some substance to it. Microfungi would have been all over its surface.

By 1532 the surface must have had a considerable layer of contaminants, the majority of which could have been removed by thorough pretreatment. However, then the Shroud was involved in a fire. Closely folded in its silver casket, the temperature went up very high, almost to 900°C, and when water was poured through the hole the cloth would have been in a situation similar to a superheated pressure cooker. The contaminants would have been pressurised into the fabric. As it cooled the water almost covered the cloth, causing the 'tide marks' obvious on its surface.

John Tyrer, the textile expert, pointed out exactly why the cloth was almost certain to give a too modern date by carbon-dating, or indeed by any other method.

Contaminants on the surface of the cloth, within the inter-lacements of the weave, on the surfaces of the yarn, and even within their twisted structures, can be removed with suitable surface actants and ultrasonic cleansing treatments. At fibre molecular level, however, the problem of contaminants presents specific difficulties.

In technical language he explains the structure of linen. Then:

As dyes are in effect contaminants, it would follow that other contaminating molecules can also enter and link chemically into the fine structure through what are envisaged as 'pores' in the fibre . . . these regions have a sorptive capacity for water, which results in osmotic forces tending to cause molecular chains of the fine structures to move apart. In so doing the molecular network is expanded and the 'trap doors' are opened to the entry of other molecules. In this way organic molecules containing carbon would become part of the flax fibre chemistry and would be impossible to remove by surface actants and ultrasonic cleaning treatments.[4]

Dr Van Oosterwyck-Gastuche confirms this:

. . . a great many materials, including textiles such as linen, wool and cotton . . . provide very anomalous C-14 dates. The high surface areas and porosity of these materials make them very efficient absorbers of all sorts of contaminants resistant to pre-treatment cleaning.[5]

Remember too that if the relic was contained in a box until 1357, except for some years in Constantinople, and was exhibited at frequent intervals after that, the excess carbon from handling and soot would have been acquired in the last 175 years before the 1532 fire.

Carbon-dating is having enough difficulty obtaining reliable results with linen connected with people and samples of people. Consider the Lindow Man and the Iceman. In these two cases, which are the most recent well-publicised cases of archaeological discoveries, the laboratories were testing material that was not exposed to the air, frequent handling, illumination by torches and being steam heated when its casket was caught in a fire, and they obtained differing and unlikely results. The Shroud's history provides ample cause for the dating to be a long way out and of differing values. The published results are extraordinary.

However, there is another factor which some people think contributed and should be mentioned. Those who believe the Shroud contained the body of Jesus Christ believe he may have affected the linen in some way.

Before the carbon-dating some believers even explained the stains as scorch caused when the body of Jesus was resurrected. The energy involved in the destruction of matter would have destroyed a lot more than the cloth had that happened. However, if there had been 13 per cent more radio-active carbon in AD 33, carbon-dating would find the cloth only 650 years old instead of nearly 2,000. Perhaps, some people of faith suggest, that could have come from the natural radiation of Jesus' body. Healers emit rays which can be dem-onstrated by Kirlian photography. The auras of Jesus and his disciples were so bright they were represented artistically by haloes.

There is a lot we do not understand about very holy people. Many have been recorded as having survived eating little or nothing for long periods. For canonisation evidence is sought that the person's body was not corrupted by death, and it is said that when their coffins are opened the bodies are still as when they died and they are surrounded by an 'odour of sanctity'. In fact this is not a medieval fantasy. In 1918 the body of St Bernadette, the visionary of Lourdes, was exhumed 37 years after her death. A commission including several physicians, appointed by the Court of Canonisation, was present. The body looked perfectly normal, with no sign of corruption. Her face, arms and hands which were open to view were white and their flesh soft to touch. Teeth could be seen through the slightly open mouth.

Those who believe that the body of someone unusual caused

the stains have one extraordinary fact in support. The blood on the Shroud is human blood. However, a normal person's blood goes black after a time. The blood on the cloth has remained red after many centuries, even surviving the fire.

That a holy body within the cloth caused the change in the radioactive carbon seems an unnecessary and esoteric explanation when the property of linen or the contamination of the cloth during its varied history explains the error in the dating. When the pretreatment can fail to detect 'atmospheric dust and dandruff' and packing materials, what chance has it with contaminants pressure-cooked within the fibres?

As the Shroud was almost certainly formed before crucifixion was banned, and in view of the remarkable coincidences between the suffering of the man in the Shroud and Jesus, the possibility of the body being his should be investigated.

The evidence of his death is contained in the four Gospels and there are considerable differences between them. How sure can we be that the written evidence is correct?

13

The Written Evidence

Christianity has more nominal adherents than any other religion, and one might expect the life of its founder to have blazed brilliantly in the records of the times in which he lived. In fact, if we ignore the literature of the Church he founded, he is barely mentioned, and the odd record that does appear may well have been inserted or altered by copyists who were his followers. It is true that he spent almost all his life in Galilee, a remote and obscure part of the Roman Empire, probably as a humble manual worker. Nevertheless, the last part of his life was momentous and he is believed to have been crucified, buried, and then to have come to life again. The witnesses to this became the firm foundation of a movement that affected the whole of the known world. For this reason, the fact that no account of his life was given by the Jewish historian Josephus seems surprising. John the Baptist was mentioned by Josephus, who should also have had evidence of the strength of the followers of Jesus. Apart from Josephus, Plutarch and Tacitus were historians of the generation after Jesus, and at first sight their silence is also unexpected.

In view of the way Christianity shaped the course of history, it is hard to appreciate that the life of this man did not seem all that important at the time. There were plenty of others like him who made claims, spoke wise thoughts, and worked remarkable cures. It was his crucifixion, death and recovery from death that supplied the spark that lit the fire. And once lit it took time to reach red heat. The beginnings of all religions are very localised. Perhaps even now some prophet in Africa or guru in India is dying, who will alter the future as fundamentally as Jesus did; yet only a few will have heard of him, in spite of the rapidity of modern communications.

But accounts of the life of Jesus do exist in the Gospels, and in this Christianity is fortunate. With many religions the life of the founder was not compiled from documents until a very long time after his death, and then in a disjointed form.[1] But first, the reliability of those accounts as records of the life of Jesus must be established.

The first point is that the Gospels were not written as histories, or biographies. They were compilations of the traditions of the Church written down for edification, worship, discipline and defence. They were not composed until decades after the events they describe, and were anonymous, being designated as gospels 'according to . . .' in the second century. Their principal authors were probably not original disciples of Jesus, although John's Gospel may include recollections by St John himself, and likewise Matthew's Gospel may possibly contain a small amount of material from the disciple of that name. St Mark is believed to have been inspired by St Peter.

The passage of a very long time before the writing down began is unfortunate, for time can warp memories as well as cut into them. There are several likely reasons for this hiatus. The first Christians were not an educated group, and this comes out in the biblical Greek in which the Gospels were composed, which has the strictly limited vocabulary of the common man.[2] The cost of materials must have mattered as well. But, most important, the early Church expected Jesus to return to earth in glory very shortly and establish 'the end of all things'. In such circumstances it must have appeared a waste of time to write down records for succeeding generations. Lastly, the tradition for the oral transmission of teaching was so strong, and memories so well trained, that there was not felt to be a great need to have a written record.[3]

The need came. The second coming of Jesus did not happen

as expected, and disciples died who had hoped to witness it. The spread of the Church, the interest of the new converts in the life of the founder, the differences with Jews and Roman authorities and several other reasons, all stimulated the desire for written records. The first Gospel, Mark's, was compiled soon after the death of St Peter, and that was probably 30 years or so after the Crucifixion. Mark's Gospel was followed by Matthew's and Luke's, and since both these authors used Mark's Gospel as a major source, they view events from a similar viewpoint: hence the three are called the Synoptic Gospels. St Matthew and St Luke also have their joint and separate sources.

The question arises, if the Gospels were not written down for at least thirty years, how much confidence may be placed in them as historical records?

It depends what is being studied. Consider the teaching of Jesus they contain. Memorisation of whole books was quite normal before writing was cheap and convenient. To assist it, teaching was carefully framed, with words selected like musical notes so that the rhythm could be remembered.[4] The sayings of Jesus in some cases turn out to be in verse when translated back into Aramaic,[5] and as well as this technique, repetition and the use of parables ensured that his message was preserved accurately. It is also quite possible that at a very early stage a collection of the sayings of Jesus was assembled and written down to act as a source book and reminder for teachers.[6] The teaching, therefore, is probably accurately recorded, although it may have been adapted slightly for the readerships for which the Gospels were written.

Some of the details of time and place did suffer distortion, however, and this can be seen from the way the Gospels differ. The cleansing of the Temple, for instance, occurs at the beginning of the Ministry in John, and at the end in the Synoptics. There are other indications of distortion. When Matthew's and Luke's elaborations are compared with the originals in Mark's Gospel, they clearly altered the stories for the particular communities they were addressing. A natural desire to exaggerate is plain, so that analysts trying to seek the truth have as one of their techniques reliance on the least sensational account. Sometimes the changes seem pointless. For instance, the title on the Cross is different in all four accounts.

So far we have only considered the Synoptic Gospels. The fourth, John's, is quite different. This is not just an account of the life, preaching and sayings of Jesus: it is more a theological interpretation of them by the author. The other Gospels were probably already in circulation, but the author of the Fourth Gospel did not necessarily draw on them. What he did was tell the story of a character, rather as a modern historical novelist does, interpreting it in terms of the philosophy and theology of the end of the first century.[7]

In John's Gospel Jesus says quite different things in a quite different language, and the turns of speech, the parables of the Kingdom, the Aramaic verse-forms, and the talk of the Son of Man are largely replaced by exalted mystic communications from a heavenly Lord.[8] Many of the stories may well be sheer invention, to provide symbolic proofs of the Messiahship of Jesus. The wedding at Cana and the raising of Lazarus are two of them, being the first and last of the seven signs. To see the extent of his inventive powers, the raising of Lazarus would have been John's adaptation of the story which had been the rich man and Lazarus in Luke. If Jesus had raised Lazarus from the dead as described by John, the incident would certainly have been reported in the other Gospels. For these reasons John's Gospel would seem the least reliable historically. Indeed, at one stage critics considered it to be valueless in this regard compared with the Synoptics, but more recently, particularly since the work of Professor Dodd in Cambridge, a less harsh view has prevailed.

Few points have caused more controversy than the authorship of the Fourth Gospel. A central argument is whether there was a single author or more than one. The writing indicates that there could have been three separate sources: the Witness, who was perhaps John the Apostle; the Evangelist, who was the main author of the work, and the Redactor, who finally revised its order and added a few passages.[9] But arguing against this is the style of writing, which is uniform and suggests a single author. The title of the Gospel assigns it to St John, but this is now considered unlikely for various reasons, principally an early statement by a second-century bishop (Papias, quoted by Eusebius) that it was written by one of St John's disciples, John the Presbyter or the Elder, under the direction of the apostle. A minor reason is that his description of himself as 'the disciple whom Jesus loved' would have been most immodest.

For the study of the Shroud it does not matter a great deal whether there was one or more than one author. The crucial point is that there is strong evidence with regard to this particular Gospel that the descriptions of the Crucifixion and the tomb in which the body of Jesus was placed may have been written down by an eye-witness or by someone with whom the eye-witness communicated. There is thus a much closer relationship with the original even than in the Synoptic Gospels.

To summarise, St John's Gospel as a whole is much the least reliable historically, particularly as far as the teaching of Jesus is concerned. The author has embellished and interpreted to such an extent that it is difficult to distinguish between what Jesus said and did and what the author thinks Jesus should have said and done. Nevertheless, among the sands of the discourses, the signs and the conversations, glisten the jewels from the memory of the eye-witness, probably St John the Apostle.

The other three gospels are much more straightforward. In them the plain outline of Jesus' teaching is clear, and their writers do not clutter up the text with their own interpretations. But the distance to the source of each item of historical observation, the number of mouths in the train of communication, is usually impossible to determine. Some matter may be only second-hand, the author writing down what the participant saw or heard, although it is difficult to be sure where this is true. An example is the story of Peter's denial, which must be true, and possibly was told to Mark by St Peter himself.

With John's Gospel the fragments that come within this

category may be recognised because they include the phrase 'the disciple whom Jesus loved', and where those words occur there are also surprising little details, touches etched into the memory of the original eye-witness, proclaiming their authenticity. The beginning of the account of the Last Supper (John 13:2–30), the Crucifixion (19:23–37), and the discovery of the empty tomb (20:1–9) all have the beloved disciple present, and although the words of Jesus contained in the passages show signs of the interpretation of the Evangelist rather than the memory of the Witness, the visual descriptions are remarkably powerful. Less reliable for textual reasons is the final scene by the lake in Galilee (21:1–25), but that may be the eye-witness again. The clarity of image in the description of the High Priest's courtyard (18:12–27) suggests that perhaps he was also 'the other disciple' with St Peter on that occasion.

The great worth of the testimony of the original eye-witness is emphasised in the text very strongly at one place, and it is a place that is remarkably relevant to the study of the cloth. Remember that the victim in the Shroud was stabbed under the right armpit while in the unconscious position, clearly to make sure he was dead. His legs were not broken. Thorough searches by Vignon in 1939 and Wuenschel in 1953 found only one report of victims being stabbed during their crucifixion, apart from St John's Gospel. In about AD 290 Marcellus and Marcellinus were despatched with a spear while on crosses because their constant praise of God annoyed the sentries.[10] The victim in the Shroud was very rare in this respect. Remember too that the blood-stains from the wound, which flowed in a watery trickle round the back, suggest that he had fluid between his lungs and rib-cage, a pleural effusion caused by the scourging. Compare these points with the description of the eye-witness in John's Gospel:

> But when they came to Jesus, they found that he was already dead, so they did not break his legs. But one of the soldiers stabbed his side with a lance, and at once there was a flow of blood and water. This is vouched for by an Eye-witness, whose evidence is to be trusted. He

knows that he speaks the truth, so that you too may believe (19:33–36).

The coincidence is extraordinary. Perhaps it *is* just possible that the man whose body left marks in the Shroud was indeed this unique historical character, Jesus Christ. A full comparison must be made between what the Shroud tells of the man it contained and the written accounts of the Crucifixion of Jesus, keeping as far as possible to the account of the eyewitness in John's Gospel, in preference to the Synoptics.

14
Making Comparisons

The stains on the cloth reveal in considerable detail the physique of the man once contained in the Shroud, as well as the ordeals he suffered and the way in which he lay while the stains developed. Do the Gospel accounts of Jesus match these details?

Beginning with the man in the cloth, the facts of his having been scourged and crucified and the probability of his Jewish origins do not make him particularly unusual. Thousands of tragic candidates fulfilled those conditions. As was pointed out at the end of the last chapter, the stab wound in the chest has much more significance, for written records suggest that crucifixion victims were normally put out of their agony by having their legs broken. Since it was normal to have a *sedile* on the cross, this method of giving the *coup de grâce*, the *crurifragium*, was administered so that the victim could not push himself up onto the *sedile* again. We know that the two men who were crucified with Jesus suffered this; and the lower leg-bones of the only crucified Jew so far unearthed—found in an ossuary in a tomb in Jerusalem in 1968—were severely fractured. The written accounts are too few, however, for this to be regarded as conclusive.

Much more important are the blood-marks round the top of the head. Putting aside for a moment the Gospel story of Jesus, there is no recorded torture instrument that could have produced such marks. Lacking knowledge of the crown of thorns, mentioned in the Gospels as having been placed on the head of Jesus, it would be extremely difficult to think of anything that could have caused those marks. It is the connection between this aspect of the torture of Jesus and those particular marks on the Shroud that gives the strongest indication that it wrapped his body.

There were other points to be deduced about the man in the Shroud from the stains. He was crucified on a cross with a *sedile*, on which he sat upright for some hours before toppling to the right, unconscious, for another considerable length of time. On traditional Christian representations of the Cross there is no such projection. This difference is important, but it is clear from early Christian writings that the exact form of cross used in Jesus' case was not described or known, and for one good reason: the cross was a symbol of shame and humiliation to the Jews, because of the pronouncement of Deuteronomy (21:23). This is why, although thousands of Jews were crucified by the Romans, the cross never became a symbol of Jewish suffering,[1] and the idea of a crucified Messiah was particularly offensive.

The Jews therefore had strong justification for failing to pass on a precise description of the cross used in Jesus' case, and the same apparently applied to the Gentile Church. Paul found his preaching of the cross 'a stumbling-block' (Galatians 5:11). Not until centuries after the Emperor Constantine substituted hanging as the state penalty could Christians, by then predominantly Gentile, bring themselves to portray the Crucifixion itself in their art,[2] but by then even the form of the cross was uncertain. They knew from the Gospels that the crossbar was carried by Jesus and a bystander, which ruled out one shaped like an X. The fact that a title was fixed to it suggested after some time that a *crux immissa*, as on Christian altars, was used rather than one shaped like a T. However, in the magnificent Doom painting over the chancel arch at St Thomas's Church in Salisbury, the cross was painted like a T as late as 1450 (see plate 28). In fact if Jesus was nailed to the Cross facing the wood and looking over the top, the title would have been nailed to the front and a simple T cross, so much easier to make, may have been used.

Artists did not know details about the Crucifixion, and although it was realised that some support for the body under the foot or crutch must have been supplied, the *sedile* was not incorporated on the Cross of any Christian sect, perhaps for aesthetic reasons.

Although the *sedile* was not recorded in the Gospels, the two positions on the cross are mirrored in the descriptions of the ordeal of Jesus. He spent some hours fully conscious and then, quite suddenly, collapsed and apparently died, remaining on the cross for another few hours before his body was taken down. The description of John, which includes the change from one position to the other, is:

> A jar stood there full of sour wine; so they soaked a sponge with the wine, fixed it on a javelin and held it up to his lips. Having received the wine, he said, 'It is accomplished!' He bowed his head and gave up his spirit [19:29,30].

The last four words have an alternative translation, 'breathed out his life', added as a footnote in the New English Bible. The expression 'bowed his head' is interesting, but no alternative is given. The Greek verb used is *klino*; apart from 'to bow' it also means 'to lean', 'to cause to slant', or 'incline', words which would more exactly have described the way the head fell into the second position in the reconstructed experiment on a cross described in Chapter 8.

And Jesus's position on the Cross? The clarity of the wounds suggests he faced the wood, but is there anything confirming this? What about the sudden move to the left, puncturing holes in his left arm just before he collapsed unconscious on the right?

On a normal cross the wine on a javelin could simply have been offered from the front. However, the clarity of the blood suggests he was facing the cross. That would not have been impossible. The wine could easily have been pushed nearly to his mouth from behind the left side, in which case he would have had to bend his head down to meet it, making just those marks on his left arm. Jesus probably faced a T-shaped cross therefore, the title nailed on the front.

Having sipped the wine, especially if it had been the vinegar which Mark and Matthew report, he would very likely have coughed and spluttered, and because of his weak state fallen unconscious to the right. Blood from those points on his left arm then began oozing across the nearly horizontal arm.

His feet must have been nailed one above the other because the ankle of one would have been in the way of the other, and the left foot was nailed above the right from the way the blood flows across the sole. This is further proof that a foot-rest was not used. The slight bend in the left knee, making the leg appear shorter than the right one, has already been noted. This is thought by some to have given rise to the wide-spread belief that Jesus was a cripple. The sloping footrest of the Orthodox cross is also believed to have originated from this.

The mystery of why the man in the Shroud did not suffer the usual fate of the crucified—of being left on the cross for animals to devour, or being thrown into a criminals' grave or lime-pit, is explained in the case of Jesus. All the Gospels report how Joseph of Arimathea, a respected member of the Sanhedrin, asked to be allowed to bury the body. He was reputedly wealthy—Matthew specifically states he was a man of means—and in John's Gospel he was accompanied by Nicodemus, who was said in the Talmud to be so rich he could have fed the entire population of Israel for eight days.[3] The expensive material of the Shroud—for Joseph may only have been able to obtain, on that Passover, 8 cubits of clothing material 2 cubits wide—ties in with the means of such men.

But there are other, more puzzling, features about the man in the cloth. For some reason his burial was not completed. He was placed naked in the cloth, unwashed and unanointed. Because it was such a disgrace to be left naked for ever, with his face covered, the circumstances surrounding the burial must have been most unusual, and without the story of Jesus' burial it would be difficult to find an explanation.

The reason is described most clearly in the Synoptics. The burial was only provisional, and it had to be accomplished quickly because of the impending Sabbath. All four Gospels mention this, but John differs in stating that the full burial rites were carried out. The next chapter discusses why he differs from the others in this respect.

The Jewish Sabbath begins at sunset on Friday evening and ends with sunset on Saturday, and in Jesus' time was observed with extraordinary strictness. The rules were laid down precisely, after interminable arguments among the rabbis, as to what constituted work and what was therefore forbidden on the Lord's Day. For instance, it was a crime to crush a flea, but you might gently squeeze it or nip off a foot. An egg could not be eaten on the Sabbath day if the greater part of it had been laid by the hen before the second star was visible in the sky. Nor could false teeth be worn, or more than three amulets carried.[4] By the time the Mishna was compiled at the end of the second century, washing and anointing a dead body were allowed on the Sabbath, although none of the limbs was to be moved nor the eyes closed.[5] However, before the destruction of Jerusalem in AD 70, observance of the Sabbath was much stricter[6] and it would be no surprise if washing and anointing a body, as well as closing the eyes and moving a limb, would have constituted work.

It is impossible to be sure about the timing of the Crucifixion of Jesus, but working from the texts most scholars now believe that he was nailed to the cross at about midday, died at about three in the afternoon and was taken down from the cross for burial at about six. The blood-marks on the Shroud, with the two separate branches of the V on the wrist, would match this chronology very well. There was then only just time to carry out the simplest interment in the tomb before sunset.

There must have been a reason for the three hours between the apparent death of Jesus and his body being taken down. According to John it was some time after the death of Jesus that Joseph of Arimathea went to see Pilate. In Matthew and Mark Joseph did not go until the evening. In Mark, the earliest account, Pilate was so surprised to hear that Jesus had died so quickly that he sent for the centurion on Calvary to come and confirm it. Joseph then had to buy the linen sheet, and it must also be remembered that Pilate was a considerable distance from the site of Calvary, inside the city walls in the Antonia fortress or Herod's Palace. There was thus plenty to be done, including provision of burial materials: according to John, Nicodemus brought with him more than half a hundredweight of spices.

Another of the seemingly inexplicable conclusions drawn about the man in the cloth is therefore answered by the written accounts of Jesus. The possibility that they were one and the same person is thereby strengthened further.

The man lay in the Shroud undisturbed long enough for the stains to form, in a trough-shaped space with soft material pillowing his head and pressing the cloth up against the soles of his feet. Exactly what shape Joseph's tomb was cannot be known for certain. It could certainly have produced the pattern of stains on the Shroud. Werner Bulst, in his book *The Shroud of Turin*, gave the dimensions of a typical tomb of a wealthy Jew of the Roman period, together with diagrams illustrating them, drawing on the researches of G. Dalmain, Director of the German Evangelical Institute in Jerusalem from 1902 to 1917. The receptacle for the corpse consisted of exactly the right sort of trough shape, with a wide rim all round. In this case, the height of the rim would have caused the cloth to fall back onto the body; but the back image of the Shroud suggests that the body was resting on sand, as mentioned in the Mishna, which would have raised it nearer the rim.

Also in the trough, according to the configuration of the stains on the cloth, were two piles of material: one under the head as a pillow, the other pressed between the feet and the end of the space.

Unfortunately, there are no written records describing how these two piles were placed in the tomb. However, in another

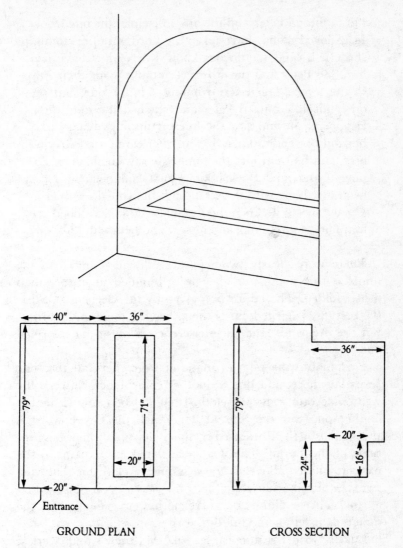

GROUND PLAN   CROSS SECTION

6   *First-century tomb of a wealthy Jew. Based on Werner Bulst,* The
Shroud of Turin *(1957).*

of those graphic eye-witness sections in John, there is a
description of how two piles of material were found there
afterwards. Mary of Magdala, the first to find the empty tomb
on the Sunday morning,

ran to Simon Peter and the other disciple, the one whom
Jesus loved. 'They have taken the Lord out of his tomb,'
she cried, 'and we do not know where they have laid
him.' So Peter and the other set out and made their way
to the tomb. They were running side by side, but the
other disciple outran Peter and reached the tomb first.
He peered in and saw the linen wrappings lying there,
but did not enter. Then Simon Peter came up, following
him, and he went into the tomb. He saw the linen wrappings lying, and the napkin which had been over his
head, not lying with the wrappings but rolled together in
a place by itself. Then the disciple who had reached the
tomb first went in too, and he saw and believed. [20:1–8]

There were clearly two separate piles of material in the
tomb at this point, and they were bundled up rather than
neatly folded. The impression given by the Greek is not that
the body was spirited out of them, leaving them undisturbed,
but the opposite. Human interference is by no means ruled
out.[7]

Presumably the piles of material were there all the time
Jesus lay there, and this is another coincidence between the
written accounts and the cloth. It should be made clear that
neither pile was the Shroud, for which the Greek word is
sindon. This is the word used by the Synoptics in their descriptions of the burial. The word translated as 'napkin' in the
passage quoted above, *sudarion*, implies a cloth for removing
sweat, while that for the other pile, *othonia*, can be regarded
as the generic plural for grave-clothes or grave-linen,[8] the
materials used for the full burial rites.

Luke's Gospel is interesting. Like Matthew's and Mark's,
it records that the body of Jesus was wrapped in a *sindon*
(23:53). However, Luke is the only one of the three to mention
the contents of the empty tomb. In a verse which not all
copyists included for some reason (24:12), after mentioning
that the disciples did not believe the women's story when they
returned from the tomb on the Sunday morning, he adds,
'Peter, however, got up and ran to the tomb, and, peering in,

saw the wrappings and nothing more.' Only *othonia*, with no sign of the *sindon*. Only grave wrappings; the Shroud had gone.

The written records do not state who placed these materials in the tomb, but we can perhaps speculate. Joseph of Arimathea, and Nicodemus if he was with him, may have taken the shroud to the tomb to carry out a provisional burial. We know they also took the spices necessary for the proper burial rites after the Sabbath. It is likely that they brought with them the other required materials—the linen *othonia* and *sudarion*. These would not have been left in the dust on the floor, where the heavy jar of spices probably stood. Instead of covering the body they could have been made into bundles, one being placed reverently as a pillow for the shrouded head to lie on, the other between the feet and the end of the trough. With the head raised on a pillow the stretched neck and the longer back image are explained. In tucking the other bundle under the feet they may have accidentally opened up the nail-wound, resulting in the jagged mark of fresh blood beside the heel. This is pure speculation, but it fits the facts and seems the most promising solution, for no one else is reported as having entered the tomb at the time of burial.

There was one other extraordinary conclusion drawn from the stains on the cloth. Although the man was in it long enough for the stains to develop, he was not there long enough for decay to begin. His body must have left the cloth when he was still alive or very soon after death. Here again the written evidence concerning Jesus matches perfectly, for he recovered and his recovery was witnessed by many people, who were able to touch his body and watch him eat and drink.

The coincidences are too great. The probability is that the body in the Shroud was that of Jesus, fantastic though it seemed when first considered. Two quite independent witnesses corroborate each other: the Shroud vouches for the authenticity of the eye-witness in John at least as much as John identifies the man in the Shroud.

13. The very large camera with which Secundo Pia took the first photographs of the Turin Shroud in 1898.

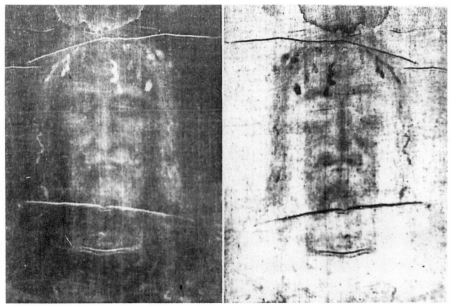

14. Negative and positive photographs of the face and head of the man on the Shroud.

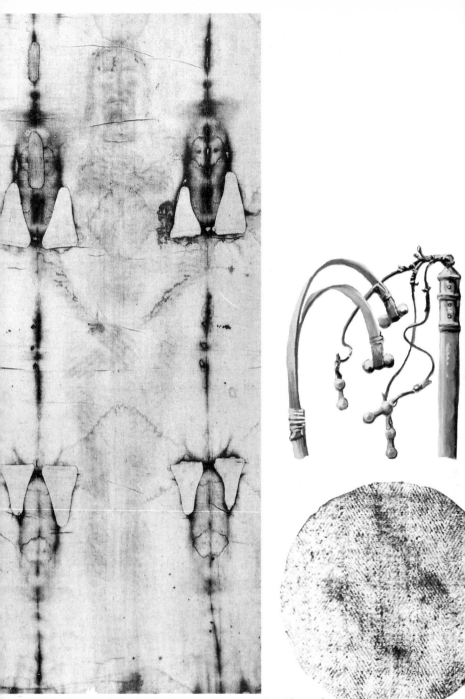

15. The front of the body that appears on the Shroud.

16. Roman *flagrums* and the bruises on the body which could well have been caused by them.

17. Roman portrayal of Jesus in a mosaic floor found at Hinton St Mary, Dorset. Fourth century. Now in the British Museum. *Copyright British Museum*

18. Christ Pantocrator mosaic on the dome of the church of Daphni. Eleventh century. *Courtesy of Ian Wilson*

Thermographic experiment to see what sort of image would be transferred from the body of a live man to a covering sheet:

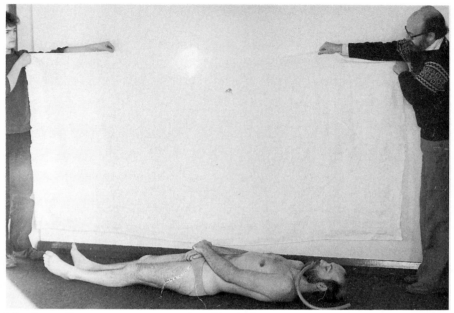

19. An ordinary camera sees only a blank sheet.

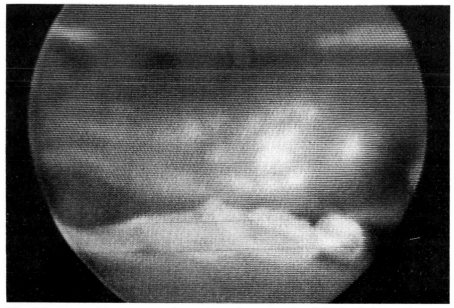

20. A heat-sensitive camera shows how the warmth of the body leaves its image on the cloth.

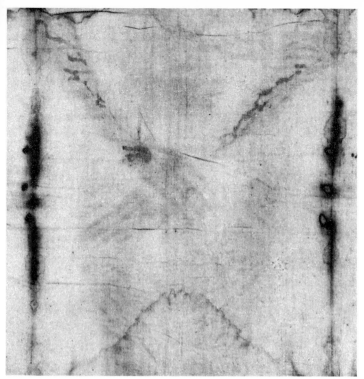

21. The arms and hands of the frontal image, showing the different directions of the blood-flows on the arms.

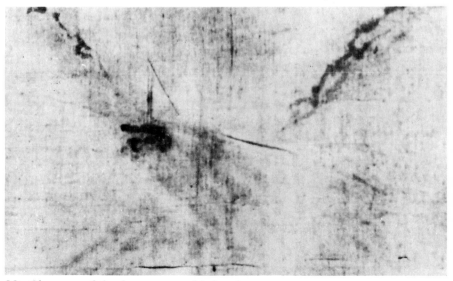

22. Close-up of the forearms and left wrist.

Experiment to show how the blood flow could have changed direction while the man was on the cross. Note that from the evidence of the bloodstains, the author believes that the man was nailed to face the cross:

23. Upright, conscious position. Note the vertical line of one arm of the V stain on the left wrist.

24. The unconscious position. The body slumps to the right, making his left arm horizontal, and the other arm of the V is now in a vertical line.

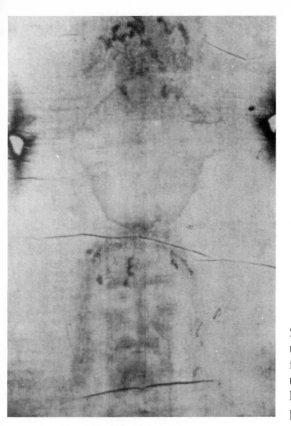

25. The bloodstains on the back of the head are far wider than those on the face. The back of the head must have been pillowed.

26. Christ Enthroned—mosaic detail from the vestibule of Hagia Sophia, Constantinople. *Courtesy of Ian Wilson*

27. The first part of the Oxford AMS testing apparatus. The solid samples are fixed round the edge of the capsule screwed into the middle of the end disc. On being ionised, carbon atoms are accelerated along this section.

28. Doom Painting covering the Chancel arch at St Thomas's Church, Salisbury. At the top of the painting Christ sits on a rainbow, his disciples below. On each side of him angels hold the symbols of his Passion, a T-shaped cross on his right with a crown of thorns on it.

15

The Body Leaves
the Tomb

'If there be no resurrection, then Christ was not raised; and if Christ was not raised, then our gospel is null and void, and so is your faith,' said Paul (1 Cor 15:13). The fact that Jesus was dead on the Cross, and then appeared among the disciples alive again, is the cornerstone of the Christian faith.

It must have happened. The spread of the new religion proves it. Nothing but the certainty that they had witnessed the return of Jesus, who had overcome death, could have turned those early disciples into the creators of the Church of Christ. The question should not be *whether* it happened, but *how* it happened.

To many, the vast majority of Christians perhaps, the 'how' does not much matter. They simply accept the event in the same way as they accept the provision of light when they press down the electric switch. Theirs is the sort of faith that is a gift. Others have to acquire it by reasoning, and therefore need to question.

For people with this urge, the standard explanation of the Resurrection poses a tremendous problem. They are told by the Church that one moment the body of Jesus was the dead wreck of a human frame in the tomb, and the next it had been transformed into a live body again. It was substance—its wounds could be felt and it needed to eat and drink—but it could pass through doors without opening them and suddenly disappear again. Questioners, puzzled by the way in which these things happened, receive a variety of unsatisfactory answers to their questions, most often: 'With God, all things are possible.'

Except for those blessed with abiding faith, this will not do. Experience and studies have shown that on this earth there are certain laws that operate. Is the only answer really that God stepped right outside those laws in the case of Jesus?

The study of the Shroud so far has shown that the marks could have been formed naturally, even if the exact chemical reaction is not yet known. The stage has been reached where Jesus' body was in the tomb, in a deep coma, on the Friday night. By Sunday morning, the tomb was empty. Only the two piles of linen remained. The body *and the Shroud* had disappeared.

One snag with the supernatural theory is obvious. Why, if everything can be explained rationally up to this point, should God interfere with the natural laws here?

The other question is, if the body of Jesus was transformed, what happened to the Shroud?

That problem has already been considered at length by scholars. It has been suggested that either *sudarion* or *othonia* could, under certain circumstances, mean a shroud. This explanation ignores a practical point. The Shroud would have been left along the full length of the trough had the body supernaturally dematerialised. The *sudarion* and the *othonia* were bundled up. If one of those was the Shroud, who bundled it up? Further, the stains show that when the Shroud was round the body, both piles of materials were already in place.

That Jesus may have been in a coma in the tomb and recovered naturally is a very old suggestion, but as far I know it has always been mooted that he would have left the tomb unaided. The forensic scientists and doctors I have consulted do not consider this physically possible. In any case, D. F. Strauss in the last century pointed out the flaw in this argument:

It is impossible that a being who had stolen half-dead out of the sepulchre, weak and ill, wanting treatment and bandaging, could have given the disciples the impression that he was the conqueror of death and the grave, the Prince of Life; an impression that lay at the bottom of their future ministry.

That leaves one alternative: the body and the Shroud were removed from the grave by somebody. Who could it have been?

Someone unconnected with Jesus is really out of the question. Body-snatchers would have had no motive in the years before artists and surgeons paid handsomely for corpses; and although grave-robbers might have taken the rich material, they would have been far more interested in the jar of spices than in the body. Neither the Jewish nor the Roman authorities could have moved it to another tomb, for when the disciples began to claim that Jesus had risen from the dead the body would have been produced immediately.

This leaves Jesus' friends, in particular the disciples. The Gospels report that most of the disciples were scattered, and the account of the finding of the tomb on the Sunday morning by St Peter and St John would make no sense if we accepted this explanation. Finally, Christianity would have been established on a guilty secret, which is inconceivable. Whoever took the body must have been a friend of Jesus, but was not in communication with the disciples.

Again the Gospels provide the clue. John's Gospel tells us that when Joseph of Arimathea[1] and Nicodemus went to bury the body on the Friday night Nicodemus 'brought a mixture of myrrh and aloes, about a hundred pounds weight' (19:39). There is only one reason why he should have brought them. They intended to finish off the process as soon as the Sabbath was over, during the Saturday night for concealment. Either Nicodemus or Joseph would also have brought the grave linen, the *othonia* and the *sudarion*. And Joseph had bought the linen sheet, the *sindon* (Mark 15:46); as time was so short before the end of the approaching Sabbath the burial would have to be temporary.

One point must be emphasised: begging the body of Jesus from Pilate and burying it were acts of very great courage and would certainly have drawn the anger of his fellow councillors. Apart from removing the responsibility for the disposal of the body from the Romans, Joseph left the body where it was vulnerable to theft by the disciples. Not only that, his actions would have been inexplicable to his peers. Jesus was a Galilean, had been a manual labourer, had falsely claimed to be the Messiah and, since crucifixion, was accursed of God. For a fellow-councillor to stoop to burying such a man would have seemed inconceivable.

The social divisions of the time were extremely wide. More than nine-tenths of the Palestinian Jews were labelled as the people of the land, the *am ha-arez*. The orthodox could not eat or associate with them, and the severity of this attitude can be judged from this quotation from the Talmud:

> No man may marry the daughter of the *am ha-arez*, for they are like unclean animals, and their wives like reptiles, and it is concerning their daughters that Scripture says: 'Cursed be he who lies with any kind of beast'.[2]

So great was the hatred of such people that the rabbis unanimously agreed that even on the Sabbath it was permissible to use a knife on the *am ha-arez*.[3] The feelings concerning Galileans would have compounded the dislike, for the qualification 'Galilean' was synonymous with a cursed, lawless rabble.[4]

It was among these outcasts that Jesus had worked, regarding them as sheep without a shepherd, and it was this as well as his failure to observe scrupulously some of the Pharisaic rules, such as washing hands before eating and misusing the Sabbath, that ensured he was regarded with animosity by the religious leaders.[5]

It would have taken considerable courage to question this disdain in the Sanhedrin, but Nicodemus, as well as Joseph, did so. John's Gospel is the only one which mentions him and he must have been a special contact. John brings out his faith clearly in the conversation he had with Jesus in Chapter 3. Another section shows his courage in standing up for Jesus. The chief priests and Pharisees had sent the Temple police to arrest Jesus.

> The temple police came back to the chief priests and Pharisees, who asked, 'Why have you not brought him?' 'No man', they answered, 'ever spoke as this man speaks.' The Pharisees retorted, 'Have you too been misled? Is there a single one of our rulers who has believed in him, or of the Pharisees? As for this rabble, which cares nothing for the Law, a curse is on them.' Then one of their number, Nicodemus (the man who had once visited Jesus), intervened. 'Does our law', he asked them, 'permit us to pass judgement on a man unless we have first given him a hearing and learned the facts?' 'Are you a Galilean too?' they retorted. 'Study the scriptures and you will find that prophets do not come from Galilee.' [7:45–52]

The background detail emphasises how extraordinary— and dangerous—it was for Joseph and Nicodemus to bury the body of Jesus. In the first place, as previously mentioned, it needed a great deal of courage to beg for the body from Pilate, an unpredictable tyrant according to the historians. But they were also putting their friends and much more at risk by performing this service to a man who was, to the Council, an accursed Galilean impostor.

If they were willing to risk so much to bury the man they revered, it is plain they would not have left his body improperly interred, and it would have been unthinkable to have abandoned it for ever in a state of ritual impurity.

It is recorded that on the Friday evening they put the body in the Shroud provisionally. The women had to wait until light on the Sunday morning, but Joseph and Nicodemus could have come any time after sunset on the Saturday.

Why did they not complete the burial when they reached the cave? When they reached the tomb and stripped off the top of the cloth, it would have been clear that the body was unlike normal corpses. To begin with, its skin would have been at a higher temperature than the surroundings. There would have been diaphragmatic breathing which might just have been visible on the lips or nose. The body might also have coughed, or jerked a limb.

What would they have done in that case? They would not have left it unguarded in the tomb. Nothing is more likely than that they decided to take it away, covered with the Shroud for warmth, to tend it and await developments. The grave-linen would not be needed, so they left it in two piles where it had been at the head and foot of the body, and the jar of spices on the floor.

That is how the mistake could have arisen. The women had watched the provisional burial. They would not have dared speak to the councillors: they were women as well as Galileans and *am ha-arez*. They could not be sure Joseph and Nicodemus would lower themselves even further and return to finish off the burial rites, so they prepared to do it themselves. When Mary found the grave empty on the Sunday morning, she reported to the disciples, 'They have taken the Lord out of his tomb, and we do not know where they have laid him.' If this is what she really said she must have meant Joseph and Nicodemus.

St John had not witnessed the interment. At about three o'clock Jesus had committed his mother to St John's care, and as soon as Jesus had died he would have hurried her from that distressing sight. He was not to know how those three hours had been taken up. He assumed the body had been prepared properly by Joseph and Nicodemus. 'They took the body of Jesus', says his Gospel (19:40), 'and wrapped it, with the spices, in strips of linen cloth according to Jewish burial-customs.' And when he saw those two piles on the Sunday morning, he assumed that they had come off the body, 'and he saw and believed; until then they had not understood the scriptures, which showed that he must rise again from the dead' (John 20:9).

The supernatural explanation was born. But the natural one is just as remarkable.

16
Peripheral Problems

There are still problems, when the Gospel accounts are studied, but none is insuperable and reasonable explanations can be found for all of them.

One question that occurs to anyone familiar with Matthew's Gospel concerns the guard. Soldiers were detailed to the tomb on the Saturday morning to prevent anyone taking the body away. How, then, could Joseph and Nicodemus have removed it?

It is quite possible, in fact, that there was no guard. Our only source on this point is Matthew, whose motives may have been either to counter rumours that the body had been removed by the disciples, or to emphasise the miraculous element. The latter suggestion is supported by his account of what happened when the women came to the tomb on the Sunday morning:

The Sabbath had passed, and it was about daybreak on Sunday when Mary of Magdala and the other Mary came to look at the grave. Suddenly there was a violent earthquake; an angel of the Lord descended from heaven; he came to the stone and rolled it away, and sat himself down on it. His face shone like lightning; his garments were white as snow. At the sight of him the guards shook with fear and lay like the dead. The angel then addressed the women . . . [Matthew 28:1–5]

There are touches here of a vivid imagination that was concerned to stress the supernatural possibilities of the scene. Compare it with Mark's description, on which it was probably based:

When the Sabbath was over, Mary of Magdala, Mary the mother of James, and Salome brought aromatic oils intending to go and anoint him; and very early on the Sunday morning, just after sunrise, they came to the tomb. They were wondering among themselves who would roll away the stone for them from the entrance to the tomb, when they looked up and saw that the stone, huge as it was, had been rolled back already. They went into the tomb, where they saw a youth sitting on the right-hand side, wearing a white robe; and they were dumbfounded. But he said to them . . . [Mark 16:1–6]

So the guard could well have been an invention of Matthew. When the tomb in which Jesus' body had been placed was discovered to be empty, rumours would have begun that the disciples had stolen it. Joseph of Arimathea was accused of that before the Sanhedrin, according to the apocryphal *Acts of Pilate, or Gospel of Nicodemus*, but such a mundane explanation of the body's disappearance would not have been acceptable to many of Jesus' followers, and therefore Matthew may well have invented the soldiers to counter the suggestion.

On the other hand it is possible, but unlikely, that a guard was placed to prevent the theft of the body and that this was known only to the source of Matthew's Gospel. In this case, judging from the other Gospels, they must have left before the women arrived at the tomb. What caused them to leave?

There are several possible explanations. The most plausible involve their entering the tomb for some reason. This may have been simply a routine check or, most likely, for theft. The quantity of spices in the tomb was an extremely valuable commodity, which they would have noted when sealing the tomb on the Saturday morning. The temptation to steal some may have occurred to them then and increased during the long day, so that they agreed to go in and remove some under cover of darkness. It would have been an unnerving venture with any corpse there; but with Jesus' reputation as a miracle-worker, so much the worse. If the body had jerked or coughed, or if they had simply seen a slight movement of the cloth from the minimal breathing, they would certainly have fled.

However, it is much more likely that there was no guard. It was Joseph and Nicodemus who rolled back the stone when they came to the tomb, and they left it open to be found by the women.

There is very little the Shroud can suggest about what happened afterwards. The man could have revived at any time, or died. As no bones were broken, a long convalescence would not have been required. Nevertheless, careful tending would have been necessary, and it might have taken perhaps three weeks for him to have reached a good, walking fitness. This may appear a considerable over-estimate, based on modern doctors' experience of pampered, overfed Europeans. A doctor who served in the Yemen for a number of years suggested that we under-estimate the strength and capacity for pain of people in that area. Living a hardy life eating millet predominantly, their bodies are much lighter than those of Western men with similar physiques, and they can stand severe injuries without showing great pain. People would walk to his surgery with wounds that would have killed their European counterparts, or at any rate left them prostrate for months. Their powers of recovery were equally impressive and no doubt the same was true of their ancestors.

The Shroud, however, cannot provide clues about what happened next, which has to be speculation based on the written records.

Unfortunately, these sections of the Gospels are not only surprisingly scanty, considering the crucial importance of the Resurrection to the early Church, but contradictory. In Matthew all the appearances of Jesus were in Galilee, in Luke they were all in Jerusalem. In John they were in both, while Mark mentions none at all. An attempt has been made to harmonise the appearances, making Jesus appear in Jerusalem on Easter Day (Luke, John) and also eight days later (John) then in Galilee (Matthew, John) and finally in Jerusalem at the moment of the Ascension (Luke); but the individual written records have to be twisted considerably to fit in with this.[1] There are contradictions even between the two accounts by the same author, for Luke, in Acts 1:3, has Jesus appearing to his disciples 'over a period of forty days', whereas in Luke 24 the Ascension apparently took place on Easter Day.

The reason for these significant discrepancies is not known. Since Mark's Gospel finishes at 16:8—the verses that follow were later additions by a different author—Matthew and Luke were unable to draw on him. They had to find their own sources, and these did not match.

As historical evidence for the Resurrection, the written records are not strong. Yet it is clear from the accounts that it was not the evidence of the empty tomb that was felt to be important, but the actual physical presence of Jesus. To sense this, one has only to read the description of the early Church in Acts. The section in John, where doubting Thomas is encouraged to feel Jesus' wounds, is equally convincing, and in Luke also Jesus is remembered as being too solid for a spirit.

> Startled and terrified, they thought they were seeing a ghost. But he said, 'Why are you so perturbed? Why do questionings arise in your minds? Look at my hands and feet. It is I myself. Touch me and see; no ghost has flesh and bones as you can see that I have.' They were still unconvinced, still wondering, for it seemed too good to be true. So he asked them, 'Have you anything here to eat?' They offered him a piece of fish they had cooked, which he took and ate before their eyes. [Luke 24:37–43]

Jesus' solidity is also obvious in the following excerpt from Paul's first letter to the Corinthians:

First and foremost, I handed on to you the facts that were imparted to me: that Christ died for our sins, in accordance with the scriptures; that he was buried; that he was raised to life on the third day, according to the scriptures; and that he appeared to Cephas, and afterwards to the Twelve. Then he appeared to over five hundred of our brothers at once, most of whom are still alive, though some have died. Then he appeared to James, and afterwards to all the apostles. [1 Cor. 15:3–7]

Deducing from such imprecise clues is difficult, but there are two fixed points from which a start can be made. In the course of years memories may become increasingly distorted, as I mentioned earlier, unless tied to fixed points such as festivals. It is fortunate in this respect that the Crucifixion took place at Passover and the triumphant announcement in Jerusalem that Jesus had risen from the dead at Pentecost, seven weeks later. There is another reason why these dates are practically certain, for from the very beginning Passover and Pentecost were the only two Jewish feasts observed as holy days by the early Christian Church.[2]

This seven-week gap has mystified scholars, for if the timetable suggested in various Gospel accounts is correct, all Jerusalem would have known about the Resurrection within a day or two. Luke cannot be right about those appearances in Jerusalem, or the suggestion that Jesus was seen by the disciples on the way to Emmaus on Easter Sunday.

If the deductions from the Shroud are correct, Jesus was recovering, in the care of Joseph or Nicodemus, for some time after his body left the tomb on the Saturday night. If any of his disciples did linger near Jerusalem after the Crucifixion, they would have left for Galilee after a few days, disappointed and distraught, convinced that their Master had been extinguished by death.

The seven-week gap makes sense in this case. What possibly happened was this. Jesus must have recovered consciousness soon after removal from the tomb. He specifically prophesied that he would be three days in his ordeal—in three days he was to rebuild the temple of his body, and by the sign of Jonah, the Son of Man was to be three days and three nights in the bowels of the earth (Matthew 12:40)—and that prophecy would have been precisely fulfilled if he came round on the Monday evening. His victory over death is celebrated on Easter Sunday simply because the tomb was discovered empty that morning, but perhaps his victory came later. Whenever he recovered, he would have needed perhaps as long as three weeks to build up his strength. He then set out for Galilee.

This is when he may have passed through Emmaus. It is no surprise that Cleopas and the other disciple failed to recognise him at first: not only were they sure he had been dead for three weeks, but extreme suffering can radically alter appearances. Farther north he may well have visited his home, for James, his brother, who was not previously a disciple, became a prominent one after this time. So to the Sea of Galilee, the shepherd rounding up his scattered sheep. Perhaps several of the disciples were fishing and saw Jesus on the shore, as in that final fragment of the 'disciple whom Jesus loved' in John 21. There is no way of knowing. The one certainty is that he did join them, and they were convinced he had conquered death and was with them again in the flesh. And in this short time with them, he charged them to establish the Church that was to spread throughout the world.

He left his disciples then. It was now up to them, and Jerusalem was where they began their ministry. So it was that after seven weeks they entered the city they had left so dejectedly and fired the Pentecost crowds with the ecstatic announcement that Jesus had risen from the dead and was the Messiah.

The recorded appearances that do not agree with this chronology may be explained by the period it took Jesus to recover and the decades that elapsed before the Gospels were written.

The unreliability of the records as regards the precise timing of these events has already been mentioned. The Evangelists were not historians, and the exact reporting of dates and times did not matter to them. The effect of the passing years on memories also has to be borne in mind. And there is a third factor: the number of people who passed on an account before it was finally set down in writing. The story of Jesus joining Cleopas and the other disciple on the way to Emmaus provides a good example. Luke states specifically that it occurred on 'that same day', the Sunday. But the Gospel was not written down for thirty or forty years after the event. The story probably passed through many mouths on the way.

Yet it reads so impressively that it must surely have happened; indeed, it was probably the first appearance of Jesus to any of the disciples. Because of this, it may have been described early on as occurring 'not long after he came to life again'. After a few years this could easily have become 'soon after'; and for this to change to 'that same day' after another decade or two is not at all surprising.

The passage of time and the passing of the message from one person to another would have caused the accounts to alter; but it was the changing view of the nature of Jesus that resulted in such alterations being given supernatural colouring. The thirst of Jesus' pious followers for wonderful details of his life and death led, as the years passed, to the production of the Apocryphal Gospels and bizarre, miraculous details were written down and believed. By the middle of the second century the story of the guard in Matthew's Gospel, quoted at the beginning of this chapter, had been elaborated to the following pitch in the Gospel of Peter:

Now in the night whereon the Lord's day dawned, as the soldiers were keeping guard two by two in every watch, there came a great sound in the heaven, and they saw the heavens opened and two men descend thence, shining with a great light, and drawing near unto the sepulchre. And that stone which had been set on the door rolled away of itself and went back to the side, and the sepulchre was opened and both of the young men entered in. When therefore the soldiers saw that, they waked up the centurion and the elders (for they also were there keeping watch): and while they were yet telling them the things which they had seen, they saw again three men come out of the sepulchre, and two of them sustaining the other, and a cross following after them. And of the two they saw that their heads reached unto heaven, but of him that was led by them that it overpassed the heavens. And they heard a voice out of the heavens saying: Hast thou preached unto them that sleep? And an answer was heard from the cross, saying: Yea.[3]

Although this and similar works were not included in the canonical New Testament, they enjoyed considerable popularity in the Middle Ages.[4] Apart from their errors of taste, they show just how much embellishment and exaggeration can be added by the pious faithful.

That same tendency must be present in the Gospel accounts, though to a lesser extent. It is in the post-Resurrection appearances that we are perhaps most likely to encounter elaborations. One of the disciples may have remembered how they were all seated in a room when, to their great surprise, Jesus suddenly came in through the door. A natural enough description, but the first hearer could so easily have misunderstood the exact message, or added an embellishing touch to imply that Jesus had passed through the door without opening it.

The stories that have Jesus appearing to the women at the tomb do not of course fit with the theory that he recovered elsewhere after his body had been removed. These stories may well have begun with rumours. Consider the situation in Jerusalem on the Sunday. Jesus, the remarkable Galilean rabbi who was also a great healer and seemed especially favoured by God, had been crucified two days before, but a report was circulating that in some mysterious way his body had disappeared from its tomb. This was exciting news, and in such an atmosphere rumours would have been quickly generated and eagerly received. His disciples had found the grave-clothes in the tomb, it was said, and were saying that he must have risen from the dead! Where was he, then? No one was sure. Apparently, his women followers had been the first to the tomb, so they might have seen him. Mary of Magdala was their leader and had been a favourite of his. Perhaps she had seen him. But the grave-linen was reportedly left in the tomb. What, then, did he wear? Ah, but it was a garden tomb, and the gardener had left some clothes there that he had been able to put on, which explained why Mary had not recognised him at first.

Such rumours could have formed easily amidst the excitement. When there was no sign of Jesus himself, and excitement lessened and was slowly transformed into deep disappointment, they would have been forgotten. But then, at Pentecost, the firm news broke: Jesus had indeed risen from the dead! He had gone immediately northwards to Galilee to be with his disciples, and here they were, spreading the news with complete conviction. The rumours were then revived, and as the belief grew that Jesus had risen mysteriously, supernaturally, these rumours became arguments for authenticity and were placed on an equal footing with the genuine reports.

In view of the change in the way Jesus was regarded during the intervening years, it is surprising that the stories in the Gospel accounts are not even more spectacular.

17

Searching Behind
the Images

It is fortunate that St Peter's first sermon, given on the Day of Pentecost, is preserved in the Acts of the Apostles. Here we can see how Jesus was regarded soon after his return to life. 'Men of Israel, listen to me,' Peter cried.

> I speak of Jesus of Nazareth, a man singled out by God and made known to you through miracles, portents, and signs, which God worked among you through him, as you well know. When he had been given up to you, by the deliberate will and plan of God, you used heathen men to crucify and kill him. But God raised him to life again, setting him free from the pangs of death, because it could not be that death should keep him in its grip. [Acts 2:22–24]

A man singled out by God. All the Jews in Jerusalem must have regarded Jesus in this way. He had lived among them and they had known and observed him as a man. A man singled out by God, as was shown by the miracles, portents and signs, culminating in his recovery from death. But still a man.

Yet, in the years to come, he was to lose that description. He was to become a part of God, the second Person of the

Trinity, co-existent with the other two eternal Persons of God—the Father and the Holy Ghost. His role, too, became more complicated. Although still a part of God, he became a man, having both natures at once. He did this so that he could suffer death at the hands of men, in order that God the Father could forgive man his other sins.

The development of this change of view is apparent in the four Gospels. The order in which they were written was almost certainly Mark, Matthew, Luke, and finally John. Although Mark was not written for at least thirty years after the Crucifixion, Jesus was then still regarded mainly as a rounded human being. But by the time Matthew and Luke were writing, and using Mark as a source, reverence for Jesus had increased.

This comes out in the texts. For example, Mark only once uses 'the Lord' in reference to him (Mark 11:3), but Luke uses it sixteen times and Matthew nineteen. Human emotions in Mark's account—such as grief and anger (Mark 3:5), amazement (Mark 6:6) and unrequited love (Mark 10:21)— are suppressed or weakened by the other two, and they omit the suggestion that Jesus' friends thought he was beside himself (Mark 3:21). These may seem petty alterations, but they are clear signs of a change in attitude.

There are other instances where Matthew and Luke do not mention human weaknesses mentioned by Mark, such as ignorance of certain points, or an inability to enter a certain town. And they add touches of the miraculous not in Mark's original stories. For example, whereas in Mark (1:32–34) 'they brought to him all who were ill or possessed by devils . . . He healed *many* who suffered from various diseases, and drove out *many* devils' (my emphasis), in Matthew (8:16–17) this becomes: 'they brought to him many who were possessed by devils: and he drove the spirits out with a word and healed all who were ill . . .'[1] Similarly, Mark (6:5–6): 'He could work no miracle there, except that he put his hands on a few sick people and healed them; and he was taken aback by their want of faith', becomes in Matthew 13:58: 'And he did not work many miracles there: such was their want of faith.' The suggestion that Jesus could not do something is subtly avoided, as is the possibility that he could be surprised. There are plenty of similar examples.[2]

The change from Mark to Matthew and Luke was considerable, but the gap between them and the Fourth Gospel is immense. Jesus is no longer a man at all. He claims he is God, and existed before Abraham. He is the Resurrection and the Life; the Way, the Truth and the Life and the Son of Man who came down from Heaven.[3] These and many other claims dissolve the humanity from him. He has been elevated right out of reach.

The passage of time is not a sufficient explanation. There must be some other factor. To see what this might be, the situation as Christianity began to spread must be considered.

The early Church was strictly controlled from Jerusalem, where Peter, James and John were the main authorities. Surprisingly, James, the brother of Jesus, was pre-eminent. The authorised version of Jesus, so to speak, was therefore disseminated from Jerusalem and this predominantly Jewish Church, firmly monotheistic, would have rejected any suggestion that he was a god. He was acknowledged as having fulfilled the role of Messiah, but although many different types of Messiah had been anticipated by Jews in the past, none had been divine in the sense of being a second God. He was expected to be a man, though a singular and heroic figure.[4] The division between him and God is shown by the ancient liturgies, which talk about 'Jesus, thy servant' and 'through Jesus Christ, thy servant, our Lord.'[5]

In the meantime, Paul was teaching a revised version to the Gentiles that was fundamentally different. And it is Paul's version that survived and shaped the Church's beliefs.

This influential man Paul had a very strange history. Starting as Saul of Tarsus, he became a Pharisee in Jerusalem, and was very much against Jesus and his followers. After a sudden conversion he becomes the founder of the worldwide church. He told others he was blinded with the truth when sent by the Sanhedrin to persecute the Jews in Damascus, but this was a flagrant lie. As A. N. Wilson points out, Damascus was way beyond the area over which the Sanhedrin had any authority, and outside the Bible there is no historical record of any persecution of the new Church by the Jews. Wilson gives a much more plausible explanation, suggesting that Paul was one of those who had taken part in condemning Jesus. Wilson suggests he might even have been the High Priest's servant in the Garden of Gethsemane. A look from Jesus, 'Why persecutest thou me?', changed his life.[6] Paul could never have admitted he had played that role.

When he went preaching abroad, his words did not have the authority of the apostles in Jerusalem, nor did Paul feel it was needed, for his inspiration came directly from God. To the Galatians he writes:

> I must make it clear to you, my friends, that the gospel you heard me preach is no human invention. I did not take it over from any man; I received it through a revelation of Jesus Christ.
>
> You have heard what my manner of life was when I was still a practising Jew: how savagely I persecuted the church of God, and tried to destroy it . . . But then in his good pleasure God, who had set me apart from birth and called me through his grace, chose to reveal his Son to me and through me, in order that I might proclaim him among the Gentiles. When that happened, without consulting any human being, without going up to Jerusalem to see those who were apostles before me, I went off at once . . . [Galatians 1:12–17]

Paul's concrete faith in the value of his calling stands out in his epistle and elsewhere. He describes himself in the heading of this letter as 'an apostle, not by human appointment or human commission, but by commission from Jesus Christ and from God the Father who raised him from the dead', and the same firm conviction in his calling shines through all his letters. But so does his sense that, because of this calling, he alone was qualified to preach the Gospel to the Gentiles. Others did not have his commission from God. He wrote his letter to the Galatians because they were inclining towards the authorised version from Jerusalem. Not allowed! 'If any-one . . . should preach a gospel at variance with the one we preached to you, he shall be held outcast.'

Paul has scant respect for the apostles in Jerusalem. He calls them 'those reputed pillars of our society, James, Cephas, and John'. And while he was happy for them to preach their gospel to the Jews, he was not going to have his Gentiles affected by it.

Nevertheless, he recognised their authority as the centre of the universal Church, and raised money abroad to send back to it. Also, as he told the Galatians, he felt that he had to go to Jerusalem to explain what he was preaching.

> But as for the men of high reputation (not that their importance matters to me: God does not recognise these personal distinctions)—these men of repute, I say, did not prolong the consultation, but on the contrary ack-nowledged that I had been entrusted with the Gospel for Gentiles as surely as Peter had been entrusted with the Gospel for Jews. For God whose action made Peter an apostle to the Jews, also made me an apostle to the Gen-tiles. [Galatians 2:6–8]

There were thus two Gospels, and whereas in Jerusalem they were remembering the man they had seen and known and who had come as the Messiah, Paul defended his authority on the basis of divine revelation. He discouraged interest in the historical Jesus in favour of mystical communion with the Risen Christ.[7] 'With us,' he tells the men of Corinth, 'worldly standards have ceased to count in our estimate of any man; even if once they counted in our estimate of Christ, they do so no longer. When anyone is united to Christ, there is a new world, the old order has gone, and the new order has already begun.' Interest in Christ as a man was irrelevant, the cruci-fixion was a mystical event, and the victim was a divine being, 'the Lord of Glory'.

Such were the differences between the two Gospels.

Acts 21 and 22 describe what happened when eventually Paul came up to Jerusalem to meet the leaders of the Church there. The whole city was in uproar, and Paul only escaped death by being rescued by the Romans and smuggled out of the city. Already there was a deep division between the first two branches of Christianity.

But soon only one survived. In the four disastrous years of the Jewish Revolt, the Jerusalem Church was destroyed. Its supreme authority over the Jewish and Gentile Christian communities loosened and then was completely severed. The group of original witnesses and disciples was decimated and scattered. The memories they had of Jesus, and there may have been a considerable quantity of written records, were lost to the world. Paul's Gentiles assumed control, and although the arguments and doctrinal struggles continued bitterly, it was his theology that provided the dogma. Therefore the destruction of the Jerusalem Church was the key to the change in the view of Christ in Christianity as a whole.

For those brought up with these developed beliefs of Christ's nature, stripping off the layers to get to the core is extremely difficult. Going back from Paul and John, through Luke and Matthew, to Mark, is the simplest part. But Mark's Gospel was probably written about thirty years after the death of Jesus, so that to get back to his real nature requires even more extrapolation, which can lead to errors. The line descends from Paul's God on earth to Peter's man singled out by God; but precisely what sort of man can not be established with certainty.

For reasons already mentioned, the best primary source is probably the teaching of Jesus, for this would have been handed on by the oral tradition fairly accurately over many years. Here John's Gospel is the least valuable, Mark's the most reliable.

In some places in the Gospels, when Jesus describes himself, directly or indirectly, one phrase is repeated by which he clearly wishes to be remembered: the son of man. It occurs eighty-one times in the Gospels, and in eighty of those passages the phrase is used by Jesus himself. In the one exception, John 12:34, the people are echoing his words. This is highly significant. By the time the Gospels were written, the phrase did not fit the belief that Jesus was divine, and the Gospel writers also knew that the title was not clear to the Gentiles. The one reason they recorded it was because Jesus actually used those words.[8] As for the meaning of the phrase, in Jewish Aramaic it often meant simply 'man'.[9] Although it is found in a different sense in Daniel 7:13, there is no evidence that Jesus used it in a similar way.[10]

If Jesus emphasises his humanity with that expression, he also makes clear that God is on a different plane. His great prayer is directed to 'Our Father in Heaven' (Matthew 6:9) and this distinction is similarly stressed when he answers the lawyer's question: 'Which commandment is first of all?'

'The first is, "Hear O Israel: the Lord your God is the only Lord; love the Lord your God with all your heart, with all your soul, with all your mind, and with all your strength." The second is this. "Love your neighbour as yourself." There is no other commandment greater than these.' [Mark 12:29–31]

Another clear indication in the words of Jesus that he did not think of himself as God appears in his answer to the rich man in Mark's Gospel (10:18). 'Why do you call me good? No one is good but God alone.' Only a man could have said this.

But perhaps the distinction is most starkly seen in the final cry on the Cross: 'My God, my God, why hast thou forsaken me?' There can be no doubt that he cried out those words. Why else would they be remembered so clearly? They were the greatest possible contradiction to the growing belief in his divinity. Nor were they muttered, as if he was reciting the first words of Psalm 22. He cried them aloud, so memorably that they are given in the Aramaic syllables that cut deep into the memories of those who heard them.

Not only was Jesus a man, but he was a Jew. He thought

and expressed himself as a Jew, and such was his faith in the Jewish beliefs and scriptures that he was willing to offer his life as a religious sacrifice. He felt that he was called to redeem his nation and intended his death to atone for its sins in the same way as the scapegoat driven from Jerusalem each year. As a Jew he felt himself to be a member of the Chosen Race, and his mission was to them rather than Gentiles.[11] This attitude shows clearly in his recorded words, which in places compare Gentiles with pigs and dogs,[12] and his instructions to his disciples to give preference to the Jews.[13] These reports must be authentic, since the universal Church would doubtless have found them an embarrassment. Long after his death, the Jerusalem Church even doubted whether his message was intended for the Gentiles: this must have been the result of the influence of Jesus during his life.[14]

Not only was he a pure Jew, but he was a first-century Jew. His medical ideas were those existing then, so that schizophrenia, epilepsy and other ailments were devils to be exorcised. The pictures painted in some of his parables, too, were strictly of his time, and this applies most obviously, if it is recorded correctly, to his descriptions of Heaven and Hell when considering whether men should cut out an offending eye or leg. (Mark 4:42–48)

Thus a man, a first-century Jew, is revealed as the basis of the portrait, but there were special aspects to him as well. There is no doubt that as a healer and exorcist he was remarkable, though others were probably equally so. Where he was unique was in the brilliance of his teaching. Throughout his recorded words, his parables, sermons and conversation, shines the inspiration that came to him from the God he worshipped and interpreted. It infected the crowds around him, and through him they glimpsed eternal truths.

The written records of the New Testament do provide a portrait of Jesus, but only the much retouched outer layer is obvious. It is not possible to strip off those layers to discover the original portrait; but a certain amount can be revealed, just as X-rays and other techniques can examine the basis of an old master painting. Underneath is the man singled out by God, and he has been described by Professor Hick in a way that could hardly be bettered.[15]

> He was a man who was intensely conscious of God, living continuously in God's presence and finding his meat and drink in the doing of God's work on earth. His life was so transparent to the divine will that he could speak about the heavenly Father with authority, could proclaim His forgiveness, and could declare His claim upon men; and the power of life flowed through his hands in healing. He was so vividly aware of God that in his presence men and women were drawn by spiritual contagion into the conscious presence of God. In this way he was a saviour to many, and continues to be so today through the living memory of him passed down to us in the New Testament and within the Christian community.

18
Roles

As we have seen in the last chapter, although the earliest Gospel was written about thirty years after the Crucifixion of Jesus, there are still enough clues to see the man behind the varnish. His words show that he was very much a Jew of the first century, conscious of his mission to his own, the Chosen Race. His deeds, too, betray his humanity: touches of temper such as the cursing of the fig tree, as well as the indication that he was not able to cure all who came to him (Mark 1:32–34). To suggest, as additional evidence, that he justified his reputation as a sinner is perhaps putting it too strongly; but the Gospels report how he was thought to be a glutton and a drinker and yet, surprisingly, they do not deny it.[1] There is a genuine human touch there, perhaps.

If his complete humanity is accepted, it is the depth of his knowledge of God that matters as much as anything. How did it come to him? Did he see God? Hear His voice?

Studying the Synoptic Gospels with this in mind, one gets the impression that Jesus had no methods of communication with God beyond those open to any man. He had to rely on prayer, and the inspired words of the Scriptures. He was a channel for God's words, in the line of the Prophets, but this does not mean he had a 'hot line' to God that allowed the accuracy of two-way conversation. He had the same difficulties, the same doubts, the same possibilities of error that all men have.

Certainly he tried to interpret God's will, but he did not give his disciples confidence in his predictions. He was known as a prophet to the people, but this was more in the sense of wonder-worker than a foreteller of the future,[2] and hardly any instances of his historical predictions are recorded. One, concerning the destruction of Jerusalem in AD 70, is suspect as the Gospels were probably written down after the event occurred. Others are obscure. However, one is quite specific: that the *Parousia*, by which was meant his Second Coming and the establishment of the Kingdom of Heaven, would occur soon after his death. Read Mark Chapter 13 to sense the whole vision. Although he cannot tell them exactly when it will happen, 'I tell you this,' he says. 'The present generation will live to see it all.' Nor is this the only place where the imminence of the event is stressed. In Mark again, at the beginning of Chapter 9, he says: 'I tell you this: there are some of those standing here who will not taste death before they have seen the kingdom of God already come in power.' The other Gospels have similar passages.

These clear prophecies, that the end of all things was nigh, delayed the writing of the Gospels,[3] as I mentioned in Chapter 13. The steady procession of uneventful days disappointed the Church, and the death of the apostles made matters worse. In Peter's second letter he says men will ask: 'Where now is the promise of his coming? Our fathers have been laid to their rest, but still everything continues exactly as it has always been since the world began.'[4]

Jesus could not hear the clear words of God—he was a man, subject to all the restrictions of men—and as a channel of communication he was inspired but not perfect. This, his major prophecy, was not fulfilled.

The other main predictions were concerned with his death. On three occasions[5] he told the disciples what would happen to him, including his being condemned to death by the chief priests and officials and his recovery from death three days afterwards. In other places he reinforces this idea of recovery after three days, the most memorable being in Matthew (12:39–40) where he says: 'It is a wicked, godless generation that ask for a sign; and the only sign that will be given it is the sign of the prophet Jonah. Jonah was in the sea-monster's belly for three days and three nights, and in the same way the Son of Man will be three days and three nights in the bowels of the earth.' Remember also the crucial claim, quoted at his trial, about rebuilding the temple in three days. This was either another prophecy, or, more likely, the same one in a different form.

Seeking inspiration through prayer was clearly a factor in such prophecies; another was study of the Scriptures, in which the word of God, channelled through previous prophets, was preserved. Jesus had a deep knowledge of the Scriptures, although there were two occasions when he either made a mistake with regard to them or his words were incorrectly recorded.[6] His study of the Scriptures led him to a conclusion on the nature of his fate. This in turn depended on the nature of the role he felt he was called upon to play.

Throughout the Gospels there is only one occasion when Jesus claims without reservation to be the Messiah, and the Gospel recording it—John—is, as we have seen, the least reliable as far as the teaching is concerned. Furthermore, the person to whom the claim is made is—of all unlikely people— the Samaritan woman. Since the Gospels were written when the very basis of the Church's faith was that Jesus had fulfilled the role of Messiah, this is extraordinary. Even when Jesus is asked the direct question by the High Priest, 'Are you the Messiah?' the answer is not an unqualified 'Yes', but rather, 'You have said so.' And when Peter bursts out, 'You are the Messiah,' in Mark (8:29) and Luke (9:20), the oldest traditions,[7] Jesus does not tell Peter he is correct but silences him.

Again it can only have been in the cause of truth that these incidents were recorded in this way. It is probable, therefore, that Jesus never made the claim, which may have been because he did not see himself as filling the role of Messiah, but his reading of scripture may have persuaded him he would become Messiah if he endured Crucifixion. One way or the other, he felt that he was singled out for a special purpose, and studied the Scriptures to see what that purpose would be.

His statements to his disciples make his conclusions clear. He was to be *Ebed Yahweh*, the Suffering Servant.[8] Through his vicarious suffering the sins of the race would be redeemed. The main text foretelling his role is in Isaiah 53, but from Jesus' words and actions it is clear that he also believed that parts of the Psalms, especially 22 and 69, were probably root sources. The rulers would take counsel against him.[9] He would be led like a sheep to the slaughter,[10] and crucified,[11] although no bone would be broken.[12] The only relevant prediction to mention death is in Isaiah 53, and this implies recovery from it immediately afterwards:[13] the others prophesy that he will not know corruption. But of one point he could be confident. If his trust in God were such that he would die to bridge the gap between God and His Chosen Race, he could not be 'accursed of God'. He would not therefore die on the Cross.

On the evidence of the Gospels, it is highly likely that Jesus expected to be crucified but that after three days and nights God would recognise him as the Messiah.[14] What form that recognition would take he could not know, but it would coincide with his second coming, which would bring in the Kingdom of Heaven.

From the stains on the Shroud and the written accounts, a picture of what happened can be drawn. Such was Jesus' confidence in his predictions and his God that he underwent scourging, buffeting, humiliation and mockery, and the agony of being nailed by the hands and feet. Greater love hath no man. After about three hours on the Cross, the doubt came. He knew he did not have the physical reserves to last three days and three nights, and there was no sign of any relief. In that awful moment his faith wavered. Suppose his interpretation had been wrong! Suppose he was really going to die, and be 'accursed of God'! From that infinite depth of despair came his cry, 'My God! My God! Why hast thou forsaken me?' Seeing his state, one of the soldiers offered him a sponge soaked with vinegar or wine. It went down the wrong way, and after an agonising spell of coughing and spluttering, he collapsed to the side, falling into a coma.

From this he recovered, as the evidence of the Shroud and the New Testament shows. What experience he had in the meantime, it is impossible to tell. People who have died clinically and subsequently recovered tell of remarkable experiences.[15] Who knows what the spirit of Jesus encountered while his body lay in the tomb? It is possible that he then had confirmation that he was the promised Messiah, and that this certainty, as well as the realisation that he had overcome death, was passed on to his disciples when he gathered them to him in Galilee.

It must be emphasised that this is all speculation; but with the background of the written evidence matching it so well, it makes Jesus a more credible figure, and a more inspiring example, than the strange God-and-man combination of traditional Christian dogma.

This personalising of Jesus also adds substance to the roles of others connected with him, particularly Caiaphas and Judas Iscariot.

Consider how Jesus must have appeared to Caiaphas. He was apparently claiming to be the Messiah, or at least so the crowds believed. If he really was the Messiah, Caiaphas and the Temple should have acknowledged his authority. But could he be? How could the Messiah be a Galilean, and the son of a carpenter? More than this, he consorted with disreputable people and ignored the Sabbath observance and other laws. God's Anointed could not possibly behave in this way. And yet how could one be sure that he was *not* the Messiah?

Caiaphas took the wisest course. Because Jesus drew large crowds he was a threat to the peace, and if things got out of hand the Romans would suppress the trouble with their usual efficiency. It was clearly good political sense that one man should die so that the race should be saved. But in addition it was good religious sense, for it tested the man's claim. If he really was the Messiah, God would not allow him to die on the Cross: it was trial by ordeal. According to Matthew (27:41–43), the chief priests, lawyers and elders even went to the place of execution to see the outcome for themselves. 'Let him come down from the cross,' they said, 'and then we will believe him. Did he trust in God? Let God rescue him, if he wants him—for he said he was God's son.' When he remained on the Cross in agony their suspicion that his claims were false hardened into conviction and their mockery of the victim increased. When Caiaphas heard that Jesus had certainly died he must have felt very satisfied with the action he had taken.

Caiaphas is pictured in the Gospels as a devilish advocate, responsible for condemning the Son of God to death. Yet he was a man, as Jesus was a man, and if his motives are analysed his actions seem reasonable. The political ends—then as now—justified the means.

The other figure who now needs reassessing in the light of this role of Jesus is Judas, and the same light can give round-ness and reality to the normal black silhouette. How could any man be a disciple of one such as Jesus for at least two years and then betray him for a relatively small sum of money? It makes no sense.

Once again the layers of interpretation have to be stripped off the relevant accounts. This means dealing, not only with the evangelists, but also with the translators. They, too, were interpreting the texts with this dark image of a wicked man before them, and this must have affected their choice of words.

The key Greek word in this context is *paradidomi* and its derivatives. In the Concordance of the Greek New Testament there are 121 entries for this word, which is translated in many ways, most as 'handed over', 'entrusted', 'given up', 'commended' and 'consigned'. Now these are relatively in-nocuous phrases, and if Judas' act of handing over Jesus to the authorities had been commonly expressed in this way, he might be thought of more sympathetically. However, of the 34 times when Judas is the subject of the verb or the noun associated with this word, in 31 cases the translation is 'betray' or 'traitor'; in the remaining three instances the translation is 'put into their power', 'handed over' and 'brought to his death'. There are 87 cases where *paradidomi* is used with other subjects than Judas, and in only four cases, Matthew 10:21

and 24:10, Mark 13:12 and Luke 21:16, is the word 'betray' used; three of those four refer to the same words of Jesus, in his prophecy of the end of all things. This seems manifestly unfair to Judas. Perhaps 'handed over', assuming he had the consent of Jesus, would be a fairer description.

The written evidence suggests that Jesus expected to be arrested by the authorities when he entered Jerusalem. Not only this, he seemed to want it to happen in order to fulfil the role suggested by his reading of the Scriptures. He was to be the Suffering Servant of Isaiah 53, the scapegoat for the sins of Israel, offering himself as Isaac was offered for sacrifice by Abraham, and trusting to be saved from death at the last moment, as Isaac was.

The Temple police tried to arrest him, as he would have wished, but the crowd prevented them. During the day the authorities could not apprehend him, so Jesus needed a go-between. As I have pointed out elsewhere,[16] Judas was the obvious disciple to pick. He was the one Judean, so by language, looks, education and contacts, he was the most suitable.

It could have been by agreement, therefore, that Judas arranged for Jesus to be 'handed over', and when that interpretation is applied to the written accounts, little points of agreement can be seen behind the veneer added by the evangelists with the developed view of later years. At the preliminary meeting between Judas and the chief priests (Mark 14:10–11), the meeting-place of the Garden of Gethsemane could have been suggested. At the Last Supper, Jesus announced that one of the disciples was going to hand him over to the authorities, and this alarmed the others who were not privy to the plan.

One of them, the disciple he loved, was reclining close beside Jesus. So Simon Peter nodded to him and said, 'Ask him who it is he means.' That disciple, as he reclined, leaned back close to Jesus and asked, 'Lord, who is it?' Jesus replied, 'It is the man to whom I give this piece of bread when I have dipped it in the dish.'

Then, after dipping it in the dish, he took it out and gave
it to Judas son of Simon Iscariot . . . Jesus said to him,
'Do quickly what you have to do.' No one at the table
understood what he meant by this. [John 13:23–28]

Judas left, as arranged. However, it would seem that the
assembly of the arresting party by Caiaphas took longer than
anticipated, perhaps because Pilate had insisted on the presence of some Roman troops. This would explain why Jesus
spent so long in the Garden of Gethsemane. His disciples,
who kept falling asleep, must have wondered why they could
not leave and go to their beds. When Judas finally appeared
with the party Jesus kissed him. 'Friend,' he said, 'do what
you are here to do.' [Matthew 26:50]

Viewing from the perspectives and beliefs of the twentieth
century, the likelihood of this account is difficult to appreciate.
The actions need to be seen through the eyes of a contemporary Jew, bound by his religion and environment. This is why
I wrote my novel, *The Final Witness—the evidence of Nicodemus*.[17]
The political situation and doctrines of the time make the
actions of Jesus and Judas believable and coherent.

So Jesus was probably handed over, with his consent, and
not betrayed. Judas, too, would have expected him to receive
Messianic recognition on the Cross after three days and three
nights as he had foretold. It would thus have been a terrible
shock, that Friday afternoon, when eye-witnesses entered the
city with the news that Jesus had died. They had seen his
chest pierced! There could be no doubt.

What Judas would have felt then! No wonder he killed
himself.

19

Imposing Probabilities

To prove beyond *all* doubt that the Shroud is genuine, and that the body which left the stains was that of Jesus, is impossible. However strong a case is made, many will refuse to believe it. Part of the trouble is that objectivity is displaced as soon as any element of faith enters into the argument.

Because of this, the first part of the book tried to avoid any mention of religion, in the hope that an unprejudiced assessment could be made of the evidence presented by the cloth. However, there is no doubt that many readers, knowing the identity of the person whose body is reputed to have produced the stains on the burial-cloth, will have seen the directions some of the conclusions were taking and refused to accept them.

After showing that the carbon-dating result was wrong, this danger could no longer be avoided. Every reader's life, whatever his beliefs, must have been affected to a very great extent by Jesus Christ, so that judgement is bound to be coloured by involvement. It is thus difficult to study the argument purely on its merits. There has been a clear precedent for this.

On 21 April 1902, the results of Vignon's research on the Shroud were given to the illustrious French Academy of Sciences by Yves Delage. After describing the visible and experimental evidence, he deduced that the stains could not have been painted but must have been produced by 'a physico-chemical phenomenon'. He then went on to compare the details of the stains with the written evidence of the Gospels, and came to the conclusion that 'the man on the Shroud was the Christ'.[1] Yves Delage was well known for his agnostic views.

The Secretary of the Academy refused to print any part of the paper that asserted the image was of Jesus, and a secret committee rejected Delage's request that the Academy ask for a more complete investigation of the relic itself since Vignon's work had been done using photographs. Outside the Academy the reception was equally surprising to Delage, most critics reacting hysterically, and Delage himself was the subject of savage abuse. In a letter to the *Revue Scientifique* he wrote:

> I willingly recognise that none of these arguments offers the features of an irrefutable demonstration; but it must be recognised that their sum constitutes a bundle of imposing probabilities, some of which are very close to being proven . . . A religious question has been needlessly injected into a problem which in itself is purely scientific, with the result that feelings have run high, and reason has been led astray. If, instead of Christ, there were a question of some person like a Sargon, an Achilles or one of the pharaohs, no one would have thought of making any objections . . . I have been faithful to the true spirit of Science in treating this question, intent only on the truth, not concerned in the least whether it would affect the interests of any religious party . . . I recognise Christ as a historical personage and I see no reason why anyone should be scandalised that there still exist material traces of his earthly life.[2]

There will be a similar reaction among many now.

Consider the evidence. The scourging by two men each holding the Roman *flagrum*. The bruising and buffeting of the face and back. The clear marks of crucifixion. The bleeding from points round his scalp as if he was made to wear a crown of thorns. The unbroken legs. The stab wound in his right side, so that when he is taken down from the cross trails of watery blood cross his back. Then read John's Gospel Chapter 19. Can there be any doubt?

The stab in his chest was complete proof of death in his time, but look at the evenness of the stains from head to toe of his body. He must have been warm along his body so his heart was just beating; he was in a coma. And as the cloth is not eaten away anywhere by the corruption of the body, he must have left the cloth still alive. The written accounts of his Resurrection show he recovered from his coma. Not only the witnesses of his Crucifixion would have known he had recovered from death, but Jesus himself.

As a record of these events the Shroud becomes the First Gospel, the pre-eminent witness, being contemporary, material and independent of the faults of human witnesses and oral transmission.

Christians firmly declare that their faith in no way depends on material evidence like the Shroud, and thus it follows that its authenticity makes no difference to them. Nevertheless, confirmation of this sort must surely help to strengthen their faith.

Theology is bound to be affected. From the Shroud combined with the Synoptic Gospels Jesus was a first-century Jew who believed he had a commission from God only to his fellow Jews. He interpreted his role as the bearer of his nation's sins who would earn God's redemption for them by sacrificing his own life. His cry from the Cross suggests that, while not claiming to be the Messiah during his life, he believed that if he offered himself up to crucifixion he would be saved from death on the third day to return as the Messiah of his nation. It was when he felt he could not last out that time that he shouted that final question.

From Paul on up to Athanarius Jesus became 'Begotten of his Father before all worlds, God of God', and so on. As a result many people turned to Mary, who had certainly suffered, to be intercessor with Jesus the divine.

The Shroud's evidence ends with the Resurrection. However, showing that the Resurrection was not supernatural, in that a physical body recovered from a deep coma, means that what happened to that body finally is now a matter for speculation. It is true Jesus still had a real, live body, a body that people could see and feel, and that needed to eat and drink. It follows that this body would have had to die finally. No evidence survives to suggest where or when that happened. But does that matter? His earthly work was completed, and he would not have dared to appear in public. Perhaps, soon after leaving his disciples, he died somewhere in Palestine, and his bones may lie there still. But bones are useless without flesh and blood, and the whole body is of no consequence unless invigorated and controlled by the spirit within.

The Shroud has been preserved until this generation could interpret it. Now is the time when assaults are being made on the value of the Gospels and the reality of Jesus. Authors use the Dead Sea Scrolls and other texts to give contradictory views of the nature of Jesus and his work. The Shroud shows the Gospel accounts were correct to small details.

Will it make any difference to the Jews, knowing that Jesus was a man and not a part of God? And that in twentieth-century terms he did not die on the Cross? Could he have been the Messiah after all? He did not die on the tree. And what excuse is there for anti-semitism when Jesus was a Jew and Judas was his main disciple?

Will it concern the Arabs? They have always believed Jesus was a great prophet who survived being crucified. Perhaps the Shroud has been preserved to speak to all the People of the Book.

What about the Christians? Jesus' admonition to the Pharisees and lawyers, 'Their worship of me is in vain, for they teach in doctrines the commandments of men' (Matthew 15:9), applies to a certain extent to the Anglican and Noncomformist churches, but especially to the dogmas of the Roman Catholic Church.

Science, History, Art, Geography and other subjects change and improve their ideas. So does Theology, but the churches fail to take the advanced knowledge into their services and beliefs. Can the Shroud stimulate a re-examination? To take a simple example, are all the 39 articles, to which all clergy subscribe, still relevant? They date from 1563. Michael Servetus was burnt at the stake by Calvin in 1553 for finding the Trinity difficult to believe in, with God no longer a Man on a cloud but Omnipresent, Omniscient. Why is He not the Holy Spirit? 'Hear O Israel,' said Jesus. 'The Lord your God is the only God.'

Sadly, the hardest task the Shroud faces is to join Christians together. Jesus gave his disciples no creed, but sects have fought for centuries about the differences between theirs.

There is a good chance that the Shroud's greatest effect will be on the large masses who are agnostic; who find the Resurrection, in particular, so opposed to normal experience that they cast the same disbelief over the whole being of Jesus. They may see in the Shroud, the uncanny meeting of the circumstances that created it, and its extraordinary preservation to this day, something beyond coincidence. They can see for themselves that Jesus Christ was a man, a special man born with the same restrictions as we have. The Shroud proves that he gave himself up to agonising suffering and Crucifixion, believing that the God he trusted would save him from death, and the fact that he survived that death is a strong indication of the existence of the God he told us about.

We can now see his face at last, as well as the signs of his terrible suffering for his fellow men. Perhaps many more will accept now that he is our example, that his words provide the rules by which men should abide rather than the Ten Commandments, and that through him, not in him, we can worship God.

Epilogue

T he gruesome nature of the research into the method of crucifixion may have upset many, and I am sorry, but that was a necessary part of the study. What is more worrying is that some readers, whose religion depends on a supernatural Resurrection, may worry when finding it was not so as we now view it. My own feeling is that one's belief should be free, and may alter. The age is a questioning one, and we should not be forced to receive our parcel of belief and take the lot. Nor should there be any form of blackmail threatening us if we do not accept that parcel.

For every one whose belief is threatened by these messages from the Shroud, perhaps many will find faith. Science education tends to push explanation in terms of material laws. However, they will need to make a further step and see that the world must also be explained in other terms as well. Just as waves are associated with all solid particles, there is a spiritual side to all live beings as well as a physical one, and it is on that plane that appreciation, hope, love and faith exist. The Shroud provides a simple, material explanation of the Crucifixion and Resurrection of Jesus, but looking beyond can be seen the hand of God.

The most important information concerns Jesus' death. Should critics read this book, I fear the eye-catching message of their report would be that the Shroud proves Jesus did not die. That would be a great misunderstanding. The right message would be that the Shroud shows how Jesus died, in his time, and recovered from death.

If this research is right and Jesus was nailed to the back of a T-shaped cross, facing it, the Gospel accounts are not contradicted, but the Cross on the altar, especially if it has Jesus hanging from the front, is not historical. This should not matter. The shape of the Cross on the altar was a guess when nothing certain was known; it has stood as a symbol of Jesus' suffering for many centuries, and will probably do so to the end of time. Christmas is a symbol of Jesus' birth, but no one claims he was born on 25 December.

Jesus being a full man on earth, and not a part of God, does not match up with Church doctrine, it is true. However, accepting this idea may make more sense and be more important for us. It means he really lived, laughed and suffered as we do. He could not see God or receive Divine guidance, while on earth. Instead he had to study the Scriptures to know God's will. He is our example of how to live on Earth.

In coming to believe this during my study I have grown to think that parts of the Creed are wrong for me. This has not worried me. Ask the members of any congregation whether they believe absolutely in the Creed—few do. Many find it hard to believe in the Virgin birth, or the Resurrection, or that Jesus was begotten of his father before all worlds. Yet we all say them if we are churchgoers on Sunday. The service, well named, is the point. The great Dr Johnson, in his *Milton*, in his *Lives of the English Poets*, said:

> To be of no church is dangerous. Religion, of which the rewards are distant, and which is animated only by Faith and Hope, will glide by degrees out of the mind, unless it be invigorated and reimpressed by external ordinances, by stated calls to worship, and the salutary influence of example.

Being a *Blue domer*, whoever invented that expression, worshipping God under the blue dome of the sky, is inadequate and, in an English winter, will glide away by degrees.

What part has Jesus the Man in the service? God is as inconceivable to us as a human being is to an aphis. For that reason we may worship the Inconceivable with Jesus, our example, as a channel for our petitions. God used Jesus as channel on earth when alive, and on the occasions He has appeared to people since, He has been in the form of the conceivable visions of Jesus and the Virgin Mary.

God probably used other examples with other races, so that their channels to God are as suited to them as Jesus is to us. Missionary work may have been damaging, as well as arrogant, in such cases. How valid can the image of Jesus, with his Caucasian features, be to an African, Indian or Japanese? They too may have had their men, specially chosen by God.

For all the People of the Book, the Shroud and the information it bears are of interest. The Vatican owns it. They should listen to experts other than Roman Catholic in all matters affecting the Shroud. For instance, conservationists are most worried that the method of storage will not prevent the growth of microfungi.

My study of the Shroud began because to me it is the most remarkable material on earth. I believe its surface touched Jesus' body; what else can have a higher claim? When carbon-dating is admitted to have given the wrong results, other methods may be tried. I have a suspicion that no scientific method will ever be absolutely certain of its age, and our belief must be based on the Shroud itself.

*   *   *

Those who study the references for Chapter 12 will notice that much of the recent material came from the Newsletter of the British Society for the Turin Shroud, of which I am Chairman and Ian Wilson Vice Chairman. Ian's first book *The Turin Shroud* was a blockbuster and translated into many languages, so he has an international reputation and keeps up with the latest news. I, and the other members, owe him a very great debt. He also kindly lent me some of the illustrations for this book. Should you wish to join the Society to follow developments through the newsletters which are published three times a year, send a cheque made out to the British Society for the Turin Shroud for £5, the annual subscription, to the Secretary, Dr Michael Clift, 9 Glevum Close, Longlevens, Gloucester GL2 9JJ.

References

CHAPTER 1

1 Damon, P. E. *et al.*, 'Radiocarbon Dating of the Shroud of Turin', *Nature*, Vol. 337, 16 February 1989, p. 612.

2 Sox, D., *The Shroud Unmasked*, The Lamp Press, 1988, pp. 136–137.

3 Gruber, E., and Kersten, H., *The Jesus Conspiracy*, to be published 1994.

4 Sox, D., *The Shroud Unmasked*, The Lamp Press, 1988, pp. 136–137.

5 Damon, P. E. *et al.*, 'Radiocarbon Dating of the Shroud of Turin', *Nature*, Vol. 337, 16 February 1989, pp. 611–614.

CHAPTER 2

1 Sox, H. D., *File on the Shroud*, Coronet Books, Hodder & Stoughton, 1978, p. 84.

2 Wilson, I., *The Turin Shroud*, Gollancz, 1978, p. 1.

3 Dickinson, I., *British Society for the Turin Shroud*, Newsletter No. 24 January 1990, pp. 8–11.

4 Gilbert, R. and M. M., 'Ultraviolet-visible reflectance and fluorescence spectra of the Shroud of Turin', *Applied Optics*, Vol. 19, No. 12, 15 June 1980, p. 1935.

5 Tyrer, J., 'Notes upon the Turin Shroud as a Textile', *General Report and Proceedings of the British Society for the Turin Shroud*, Autumn 1979–Summer 1981, p. 25.

6 Raes, G., Appendix B—Analysis Report, *Report of the Turin Commission on the Holy Shroud*, 1976, p. 83.

7 Tyrer, J., *op. cit.*, p. 30.

8 Wilcox, R. K., *Shroud*, Corgi Books, 1978, p. 45.

9 Tyrer, J., 'Looking at the Turin Shroud as a Textile', *Textile Horizons*, December 1981, p. 20.

10 Humber, T., *The Fifth Gospel*, Pocket Books, 1974, p. 28.

11 Walsh, J., *The Shroud*, Star Books, W. H. Allen, 1979, p. 101.

12 Sox, H. D., *The Image on the Shroud*, Unwin Paperbacks, 1981, p. 76.

13 Tyrer, J., *op. cit.* (9), p. 21.

14 Stevenson, K. E., and Habermas, G. R., *Verdict on the Shroud*, Robert Hale, 1982, p. 26.

15 Rinaldi, P. M., *The Man in the Shroud*, Futura, 1974, p. 58.

16 Schwalbe, L. A., and Rogers, R. N., 'Physics and Chemistry of the Shroud of Turin', *Analytica Chimica Acta*, 135 (1982), 3–49, p. 44.

17 Tyrer, J., *op. cit.* (5), p. 25.

18 Walsh, J., *op. cit.*, p. 30.

19 *Ibid.*, p. 9.

20 Crispino, D., 'The Report of the Poor Clare Nuns, Chambéry, 1532', *Shroud Spectrum International No. 2*, Indiana Center for Shroud Studies, March 1982, p. 24.

CHAPTER 3

1 Fossatti, L., 'Copies of the Holy Shroud', *Shroud Spectrum International*, Indiana Center for Shroud Studies, September 1984, No. 12, p. 23.

2 *Ibid.*, pp. 8 and 10.

3 Wilson, I., *the Turin Shroud*, Gollancz, 1978, p. 175.

4 Quoted in Wilson, I., *op. cit.*, p. 171.

5 Bryant, A., *The Age of Chivalry*, The Reprint Society, 1965, p. 414.

6 Quoted in Wilson, *op. cit.*, p. 144.

7 Robert di Clari, *The Conquest of Constantinople*, trs. E. H. McNeal (New York: Columbia Press, 1936) quoted in Wilson, I, *The Turin Shroud*, Gollancz, 1978, p. 76.

8 Wilson, I., *The Turin Shroud*, Gollancz, 1978, p. 163.

9 Barber, M., *The Trial of the Templars*, Cambridge University Press, 1978, quoted p. 241.

10 Wilson, I., *British Society for the Turin Shroud Newsletter*, 35, Aug/Sept 1993, p. 14.

11 Bishop Eusebius of Caesarea, *The History of the Church*, p. 325.

12 Humber, T., *The Fifth Gospel*, Pocket Books, 1978, p. 72.

13 Wilson, I., *The Turin Shroud*, Gollancz, 1978, Appendix A.

CHAPTER 4

1 *The Report of the Turin Commission on the Holy Shroud*, 1976, p. 20.
2 Schwalbe, L. A., and Rogers, R. N., 'Physics and Chemistry of the Shroud of Turin', *Analytica Chimica Acta*, 135 (1982), 3–49, p. 7.
3 *Ibid.*, p. 10. Sox, H. D., *The Image on the Shroud*, Unwin Paperbacks, 1981, p. 90.
4 Schwalbe, L. A., and Rogers, R. N., *op. cit.*, p. 43.
5 *Ibid.*, p. 11.
6 *Ibid.*, pp. 22–24.
7 Bollone, Jorio and Massaro, 'Identification of the Group of the Traces of Human Blood on the Shroud', *Shroud Spectrum International No. 6*, Indiana Center for Shroud Studies, March 1983.
8 *Ibid.*

CHAPTER 5

1 Memorandum of Pierre D'Arcis, Bishop of Troyes, to the Avignon Pope Clement VII (written late 1389), trs. from the Latin by the Rev. Herbert Thurston and published in 'The Holy Shroud and the Verdict of History', *The Month*, C1 (1903), pp. 17–29
2 Dreisbach, Revd. K., Letter to *British Society for the Turin Newsletter*, No. 25, April/May 1990.
3 Sox, H. D., *The Image on the Shroud*, Unwin Paperbacks, 1981, p. 20.
4 *Ibid.*, p. 34.
5 Schwalbe, L. A., and Rogers, R. N., 'Physics and Chemistry of the Shroud of Turin', *Analytica Chimica Acta*, 135 (1982), 3–49, pp. 11–16.
6 Heller, J. H., and Adler, A. D., 'A Chemical Investigation of the Shroud of Turin', *Canadian Journal of Forensic Science*, Vol. 14. No. 3 (1981), pp. 81–100.
7 Cahill, T. A., *et al*. 'The Vinland Map Revisited: New Compositional Evidence of its Inks and Parchment', *Analytical Chemistry*, Vol. 53, No. 6, 1987 March 15, pp. 828–832.
8 Wilson I., *op. cit.*, p. 10.
9 Tyrer, J., 'Notes upon the Turin Shroud as a Textile', *General Report and Proceedings of the British Society for the Turin Shroud*, Autumn 1979–Summer 1981, p. 29.

CHAPTER 6

1 Vignon, P., *The Shroud of Christ*, Constable, 1902, p. 29.
2 *Ibid.*, p. 40.
3 Hynek, R. W., *The True Likeness*, Sheed & Ward, 1951, p. 52.
4 Vignon, P., *op. cit.*, p. 137.
5 *Ibid.*, p. 169.

CHAPTER 7

1 Stevenson, K. E., and Habermas, G. R., *Verdict on the Shroud*, Robert Hale, 1982, p. 89.
2 Wilcox, R. K., *Shroud*, Corgi, 1978, p. 136.
3 Newitt, C., and Green, M. A., 'A Thermographic Study of Surface Cooling of Cadavers', *Journal of the Forensic Science Society*, 19. 197 (1979), pp. 179–181.
4 Hardy, J. D., and Du Bois, E. F., 'Basal Metabolism, Radiation, Convection and Vaporization at Temperatures of 22 to 35°C', *The Journal of Nutrition*, Vol. 15, No. 5 (1938), pp. 480–486.

CHAPTER 8

1 Barton, N. J., 'Without Thumbs . . . a Theory', *General Report and Proceedings of the British Society for the Turin Shroud*, Autumn 1979.
2 Humber, T., *The Fifth Gospel*, Pocket Books, 1974, p. 125.
3 Hengel, M., *Crucifixion*, SCM, 1977, p. 155.
4 *Ibid.*, p. 26.
5 *Ibid.*, p. 30.
6 *New Bible Dictionary*, Inter Varsity Fellowship, 1962, p. 282.
7 Willis, D., 'Did He Die on the Cross?', *The Ampleforth Journal*, 74 (1969), p. 33.
8 Barbet, P., *A Doctor at Calvary*, Image Books, 1963, p. 43.

CHAPTER 9

1 Rinaldi, P. M., *The Man in the Shroud*, Futura, 1974, p. 84.
2 Humber, T., *The Fifth Gospel*, Pocket Books, 1974, p. 29.
3 Wilson, I., *The Turin Shroud*, Gollancz, 1978, p. 21.
4 Humber, T., *op. cit.*, p. 43.
5 Wilson, I., *op. cit.*, p. 32.
6 Wilcox, R., *Shroud*, Corgi Books, 1978, p. 133.
7 Robinson, J. A. T., 'The Shroud and the New Testament' in *Face to Face with the Turin Shroud*, ed. Peter Jennings, Mayhew-McCrimmon and A. R. Mowbray, 1978, p. 71.

8 Humber T., *op. cit.*, p. 29.
9 *Ibid.*, p. 52.
10 O'Rahilly, A., *The Burial of Christ*, Cork University Press, 1942, p. 1.
11 *Ibid.*, p. 6.
12 Humber T., *op. cit.*, p. 53.
13 O'Rahilly, A., *op. cit.*, p. 13.

CHAPTER 11
1 e.g. Hedges, R. E. M., and Gowlett, J. A. J., 'Radiocarbon Dating by Accelerator Mass Spectrometer', *Scientific American*, Vol. 254, No. 1 (1986), pp. 100–107.
2 Wilson I., *British Society for the Turin Shroud Newsletter*, No. 21, Jan/Feb 1989, p. 4.
3 *Ibid.*, No. 30, Dec/Jan 1992, p. 8.
4 *Ibid.*, No. 14, Sept 1986, pp. 3, 4.
5 *Ibid.*, No. 31, April/May 1992, pp. 5–7.
6 *Ibid.*, No. 25, April/May 1990, p. 13.
7 *Ibid.*, No. 28, April/May 1991, pp. 9, 10.
8 Coghlan, A., 'Unexpected errors affect dating techniques', *New Scientist*, 30 September 1989, p. 26.

CHAPTER 12
1 Sox, D., *The Shroud Unmasked*, The Lamp Press, 1988, p. 138.
2 Wilson, I., *British Society for the Turin Shroud*, Newsletter No. 30, Dec 1991/Jan 1992, pp. 5–8.
3 Van Oosterwyck-Gastuche, M. C., 'Another Contribution to the Radiocarbon Dating Debate', *British Society for the Turin Shroud Newsletter*, No. 36, Dec 1993/Jan 1994, p. 10.
4 Tyrer, J., *Is it really a fake?* Article sent round to friends, 1989.
5 Van Oosterwyck-Gastuche, M. C., *op. cit.*, p. 7.

CHAPTER 13
1 Grant, F.C., *The Gospels—Their Origin and Growth*, Faber & Faber, 1965, p. 25.
2 Leon-Dufour, X., *The Gospels and the Jesus of History*, Collins, 1968, p. 25.
3 Grant, F. C., *op. cit.*, pp. 26, 29.
4 Gerhardsson, B., *The Origin of the Gospel Traditions*, SCM, 1979, p. 19.
5 Cupitt, D., and Armstrong P., *Who Was Jesus?* BBC, 1997, p. 53.

6 Dodd, C. H., *The Founder of Christianity*, Collins, 1972, p. 20.

7 Guy, R. A., *The Study of the Gospels*, Macmillan, 1967, p. 43.

8 Cupitt, D., and Armstrong, P., *op. cit.*, p. 56.

9 Grant, F. C., *op. cit.*, p. 176.

10 Meacham, W. 'The Authentication of the Turin Shroud: An Issue in Archaeological Epistemology', *Current Archaeology*, Vol. 24, No. 3, June 1983, p. 292.

CHAPTER 14

1 Hengel, M., *Crucifixion*, SCM, 1977, p. 85.

2 Priestland, G., *Yours Faithfully*, Collins, 1979, p. 133.

3 Daniel-Rops, *Jesus in His Time*, Eyre & Spottiswoode, 1955, p. 161.

4 *Ibid.*, pp. 61, 212.

5 O'Rahilly, A., *The Burial of Christ*, Cork University Press, 1942, p. 32.

6 Leon-Dufour, X., *The Gospels and the Jesus of History*, Collins, 1968, p. 69.

7 Robinson, J. A. T., *The Human Face of God*, SCM, 1973, p. 136.

8 Robinson, J. A. T., 'The Shroud and the New Testament' in *Face to Face with the Turin Shroud*, ed. Peter Jennings, Mayhew-McCrimmon and A. R. Mowbray, 1978, p. 70.

CHAPTER 15

1 Morison, F., *Who Moved the Stone?* Faber & Faber (1944 ed.), p. 92.

2 Vermes, G., *Jesus the Jew*, Fontana/Collins, 1976, pp. 54, 55.

3 Daniel-Rops, *Jesus in His Time*, Eyre & Spottiswoode, 1955, p. 134.

4 Vermes, G., *op. cit.*, p. 33.

5 Metzger, B., *The New Testament, its Background, Growth and Content*, Lutterworth Press, 1969, p. 46.

CHAPTER 16

1 Leon-Dufour, X., *The Gospels and the Jesus of History*, Collins, 1968, pp. 255–257.

2 *Ibid.*, p. 260.

3 James, M. R., *The Apocryphal New Testament*, Oxford University Press, 1953, p. 92.

4 Daniel-Rops, *Jesus in His Time*, Eyre & Spottiswoode, 1956, pp. 25–28.

CHAPTER 17

1 Metzger, B., *The New Testament, its Background, Growth and Content*, Lutterworth Press, 1969, p. 80.
2 Mitton, C. L., *Jesus: The Fact behind the Faith*, Mowbray, 1975, pp. 42–46.
3 Hanson, R. P. C., 'The unexamined assumption of most Christian believers', *The Times*, 10 June 1978.
4 Brandon, S. G. F., *The Fall of Jerusalem and the Christian Church*, SPCK, 1951, p. 79.
5 Cullman, O., *The Christology of the New Testament*, SCM, 1963, p. 75.
6 Wilson, A. N., *Jesus*, Sinclair-Stevenson, 1992, pp. 26f., 204.
7 Brandon, S. G. F., *The Trial of Jesus of Nazareth*, Batsford, 1968, pp. 18, 19.
8 Filson, F. V., *A New Testament History*, SCM, 1965, p. 78.
9 Dodd, C. H., *The Founder of Christianity*, Collins, 1871, p. 111.
10 Vermes, G., *Jesus the Jew*, Fontana/Collins, 1976, p. 185.
11 Dodd, C. H., *op. cit.*, Chapter 5.
12 Matthew 7:6; Matthew 15:26.
13 Matthew 10:5,6; Matthew 15:24.
14 Vermes, G., *op. cit.*, p. 49. Acts 10.
15 Hick, J., 'Changing views of the uniqueness of Christ', *The Times*, 11 October 1975.

CHAPTER 18

1 Robinson, J. A. T., *The Human Face of God*, SCM, 1973, pp. 97–98.
2 Vermes, G., *Jesus the Jew*, Fontana/Collins, 1973, Chapter 4.
3 Grant, F. C., *The Gospels—Their Origin and Growth*, Faber & Faber, 1965, pp. 29, 33.
4 II Peter 3:4.
5 In Mark see 8:31, 9:31 and 10:33–34, and there are parallel texts.
6 Mark 2:26 and Matthew 23:35. See Brown, R. E. *Jesus, God and Man*, Chapman, 1967, pp. 51–54.
7 Brown, R. E., *op. cit.*, p. 82.
8 Cullmann O., *The Christology of the New Testament*, SCM, 1963, pp. 61–69.
9 Psalm 22:2 and Psalm 41:5 and 7.
10 Isaiah 53:7.
11 Psalm 22:16.
12 Psalm 22:17.

13 Isaiah 53:9–10.
14 Hoare, R. P., *The Testimony of the Shroud*, Quartet, 1978, Chapter 10.
15 Ritchie, G., *Return from Tomorrow*, Kingsway, 1978. Also Moody, R. A., *Life after Life*, Bantam Books, 1976.
16 Hoare, R. P., *op. cit.*, pp. 103–109.
17 Hoare, R. P., *The Final Witness*, Crest Books, 23 Elm Grove Road, Salisbury. Copies are still available by post @ £5.

CHAPTER 19
 1 Walsh, J., *The Shroud*, W. H. Allen, 1979, pp. 75–76.
 2 Humber, T., *The Fifth Gospel*, Pocket Books, 1974, pp. 109–111.

Index

Numbers in italics refer to illustration numbers